DEEP ROOTS

WILD BRANCHES

DEEP
ROOTS
WILD
BRANCHES

Revitalizing the Church in the Blended Ecology

Michael Adam Beck

 Seedbed

Printed in the United States of America

Image on page xiii created by Wilma Ivelisse Reyes
Cover design by Strange Last Name
Page design by PerfecType, Nashville, Tennessee

Beck, Michael Adam
    Deep roots, wild branches : revitalizing the church in the blended ecology / Michael Adam Beck. – Franklin, Tennessee : Seedbed Publishing, ©2019.

    pages ; cm.

    ISBN 9781628246223 (paperback)
    ISBN 9781628246230 (Mobi)
    ISBN 9781628246247 (ePub)
    ISBN 9781628246254 (uPDF)

    1. Church renewal. 2. Missional church movement. 3. Emerging church movement. I. Title.

BV600.3.B42 2019   262/.26   2019932034

SEEDBED PUBLISHING
Franklin, Tennessee
seedbed.com

DEDICATION

To my beautiful bride, copastor, and partner on the mission field and life, Jill Beck. You awakened me with your faithful love.

To all eight of our beloved children in this blended, chaordic organism called the Beck family: Emily, Ariel, Kaitlyn, Caitlin, Donald, Michael Jr., Alexander, and Angel.

To our grandchildren, Jaxon, Gabriella, and Aurora, for the light you have brought to our lives.

To the people called Methodists, who invited a little orphan boy to the potluck table of grace and raised me in a community of love and forgiveness.

To the WildOnes and my fellow pioneers of Fresh Expressions US, for the laughter and the tears we have shared, laboring in Christ on the new missional frontier.

Contents

Parental Discretion Advised

When we were young, most things we truly desired came with the standard parental discretion advisory. Of course, this made us want it even more! The idea of the parental advisory was to give parents the choice if they wanted to allow their children to be exposed to something with violence, sex, or explicit lyrics.

I have always wanted to create a custom Bible with a parental discretion advisory label on the front in the hopes it would compel my children to read it. I mean, if anything in this world needs a parental discretion warning it's the Bible, right? Sex, alcoholism, violence, incest, polygamy, bestiality, genocide, humans beating their fists on the chest of God, children bashed on rocks, epic disasters; it's all in there. Who would let their kids read that stuff or watch that movie or listen to that soundtrack? This book will engage the Bible in a fresh way, so beware.

However, I start with this notice really because I want you to understand that what you hold in your hands is dangerous . . . like dynamite. Dynamite is a peculiar thing.

It can be both highly destructive or highly effective at accomplishing an impossible task. It really depends on the intent of the wielder. For instance, you can use dynamite in a terrorist attack to kill innocent people or you can use it to blow a tunnel through a mountain so you can drive a train through it. What I propose here is explosively hopeful. This dynamite-like optimism could destroy the imaginative gridlock of a "we've always done it that way before" church. It could turn obstacles to renewal into shrapnel and it could blow a community apart so that God can reconfigure it in a splendid new creation mosaic.

One thing to be cognizant of is the importance of knowing who is the "parent" wielding the power of discretion in your church, denomination, network, or community. Your episcopal leader, for instance, may not want you reading this. It might be a threat to the established bureaucracy. If you are a clergy person, you probably answer to some human authority, be it a board or a bishop. They might not like it when I suggest that you must understand and reclaim your identity as a mini-bishop and see your community as a kind of microcosm for what has been traditionally known as a conference, diocese, district, and so on. They may certainly get heartburn when you start ordaining/commissioning local missionaries to your community and planting churches willy-nilly all over the town. When you start releasing wolves into artificial ecosystems, it's messy. Trophic cascades cannot be managed or institutionalized.

If you are just a normal Christian (I dislike the entire clergy/laity distinction because of its weak basis in Scripture), your "momma/daddy" might be your pastor. They may be uncomfortable when you begin to take your place in the "priesthood" of all believers (1 Peter 2:5) and understand yourself as an apostle, prophet, evangelist, pastor, and teacher to your community (Eph. 4:11). If your ecclesial parental figure has a realistic view of the new missional frontier they will embrace, support, and give permission. They will begin to cherish your contribution as you join the Holy Spirit's disruptive work in the world. We need ordinary heroes like you, not gurus and professionals.

Unfortunately, some of you who are in unhealthy leadership dynamics may have to shoplift this material, hide it in your underwear drawer, or download it cautiously. This is your parental discretion warning: caution—ingredients could be explosively hopeful; handle with care.

The Central Vision:
A Tree of Life

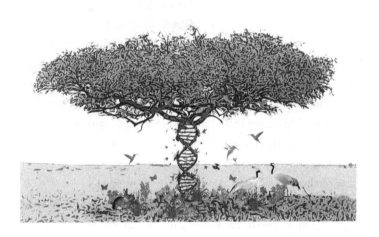

I want to invite you to a picnic. This is an invitation to sit together beneath the tree of life and share a meal. The picnic is three courses and the book you hold in your hands is the appetizer. I invite you to stay for each portion of the meal, but it's my hope that the appetizer will be delightful enough that you can ingest a new vision for your local church.

The appetizer offers bite-sized pieces of what will be served in full portions in the main course. Yet, there is enough sustenance here for local churches to get started planting their own gardens.

The story of creation features a "tree of life" (Gen. 2:9). When that paradise scenario becomes polluted with sin, we lose access to this tree that we "might reach out [our] hand and take also from the tree of life, and eat, and live forever" in some undead state (Gen. 3:22). Later, we learn of another tree, from which a "cursed" one hung, to redeem us from the pollution of sin (Gal. 3:13). The prophets and pagan kings dreamed of a tree in which life would find shade and birds shelter (Dan. 4:1–12). Jesus takes up that language to describe the small mustard-seed beginnings that bring that kingdom tree into being (Matt. 13:31–32). Our story ends back at that tree in an urban garden. The story of new creation features again the "tree of life," where all the tribes now gather in peace to taste its fruit (Rev. 22:2).

Perhaps most relevant to our topic of cultivating new communal ecosystems amidst declining congregations is Ezekiel's prophecy, "I dry up the green tree and make the dry tree flourish" (Ezek. 17:24). Our story is centered on a God who restores creation around the tree, who can make "dry tree[s] flourish." To begin our journey, I want to offer you a guiding vision. This is a remixed metaphor of the old/new tree story. This controlling image will guide us forward.

The central image is that of a large and beautiful tree in the middle of the desert. Somehow this ancient and resilient structure is standing fully alive in stark contrast to the void of life all around.

As you behold this awe-inspiring organism, you notice in the shade beneath its elegant branches little shoots of life emerging from the root ball. These nascent organisms spring wildly into life, forming a tapestry of color all around the tree roots. These new flowers, plants, and vines cannot exist on their own; they need the shade of the tree. Somehow, they also give life to the tree. This is a symbiotic relationship.

The birds shelter and sing in its branches. Other strange life-forms find a new home. This is the vision of the blended ecology way. It's a resurrection image, a subversive ecosystem in the hostile death-dealing desert. It's an image of generativity—life exploding forth profusely in wild ways—on the backdrop of scarcity. It defies logic and rationality and invites us to turn to wonder. The tree and the emerging network of life is creating an entirely new environment in the middle of the desert. It's a counter-narrative to the greater story of waterless, lifeless void.

The tree is fundamentally a both/and image. It is an organism of Deep Roots *and* Wild Branches. Rooted in God's faithful activity in the past *and* growing wildly toward God's promised future manifesting in the present. In a space of liminality, a threshold between times, Paul uses this very metaphor to describe the composite nature of the church (Rom. 11:17–24). As communal life in Jesus began to take on new forms among the Gentiles, Paul describes this transformation as grafting, "what is by nature a wild olive tree and grafted, contrary to nature, into a cultivated olive tree" (Rom. 11:24).

For us then, the tree itself is an image of the *inherited* church, with its rootedness and depth. It possesses a resilient strength that will not submit to the parched context. The wild new life-forms, dependent on the tree's shade and nourishing root system, are the *emerging* forms of church. These are the fresh expressions tethered to and dependent upon the inherited structure. There is a life-giving exchange happening between the inherited and emerging dynamic, imparting fresh air and creating new life where there was none before.

My doctoral mentor and my "Paul" in the faith, Dr. Leonard Sweet, says that what the Spirit is up to in the new reformation is not about making a better church, but making a better world. I hope this book will encourage you to join us to start planting the seeds of a new tomorrow by cultivating flourishing nascent ecosystems centered around the churches in your community today.

In the world of urban planning, refitting polluted and decaying cities with green technologies for a sustainable future is called *retrofitting*. In the world of revitalization, rewiring declining congregations to join the Spirit's work of transforming communal ecosystems is called *futurefitting*.

Let's begin futurefitting your local church in the blended ecology way for life at the tree!

Picnic Talk

I've structured this pocket-sized book in a way that your team can work through the chapters together and hopefully get started cultivating the blended ecology in your local church. At the end of each chapter, I'll offer some questions to prime discussions and later some interactive tools. I invite you to imagine what it will sound like sitting in the shade beneath the tree of life in the new creation. Perhaps playing a track of nature sounds would set the mood? Or better yet, find a place in your community (park, nature trail, playground) and have an actual picnic together as you talk! Try to practice the discipline of presence and listening as each person shares.

PART ONE

The New Ecosystem

Why the Blended Ecology?

Trailer

Jesus took my broken life and revitalized it. This is partly the *why* of this book. I believe churches can experience new life in the same way individuals can. In a landscape where fewer people know the love of God revealed in Jesus Christ, I believe we need every church in every community engaging the mission field to awaken people to that love. Just as we must be willing to go through a journey of death and resurrection, so must our churches.

In May 2012, my wife, Jill, and our blended family of eight children visited the church we would be serving that July. Wildwood United Methodist Church of Wildwood, Florida. Our family of ten nearly doubled the congregation that first Sunday! There were around thirty people in worship, the majority of whom were chronologically mature (precious saints more than eighty years old, sustaining the church with their blood, sweat, and tears). This was not a vibrant season in the life of our church.

During the apex of our history, from the early 1950s and into the 1970s, more than five hundred souls worshiped at Wildwood each Sunday. By 1998, Wildwood reported 240 people in worship. In 2008, just ten years later, Wildwood reported 127 people in worship. In 2012, Wildwood was in a conversation about closure or merger with a nearby thriving mega church. Although the congregation has existed on the same property for almost 140 years, an initial door-to-door canvass of the surrounding neighborhood revealed that residents living within visual proximity did not know of Wildwood UMC.

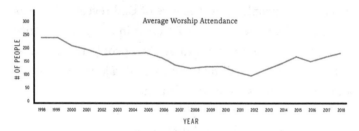

Wildwood UMC, Average Worship Attendance 1998-2018

Today, around two hundred WildOnes (what we call ourselves) worship regularly in our two different services on Sunday, as well as an additional one hundred in a third service of our sister church, God's Glory Ministries Inc. We share our space and partner in various ways with this African American congregation in the Pentecostal stream.

This is quite remarkable, being that Wildwood was founded in 1881 as a Methodist Episcopal South congregation (a denomination resulting from the split over slavery in 1844). Wildwood looks very different these days. More and more, we are blending our two church families together; this is a sign of Jesus' resurrection power at work.

On one hand, we are a traditional United Methodist congregation with deep roots, a long history, and all the typical offerings: office hours, Bible studies, United Methodist Women, quilters guilds, pews, bulletins, hymnals, candles, and all the smells and bells. In a typical week our pastoral team has all the expectations of a traditional parish to meet. In just one day, we have been asked to be sound technicians, mechanics, janitors, administrators, interventionists, architects, fund-raising gurus, counselors, and preachers extraordinaire.

However, also in a normal week, some quite wild and not-so-traditional things are occurring as many more people are also gathering in the thirteen various fresh expressions. These micro-churches gather around the risen Jesus in tattoo parlors, Mexican restaurants, community centers, dog parks, Yoga studios, libraries, running tracks, and makeshift salons. These little communities of Jesus are littered throughout Wildwood like green spaces to our ecosystem. We are very much a presence in the lives of people where they do life. Disciples are being made. We are witnessing an emergence—fragmented pieces being blended together into a wonderful new creation mosaic—a community of resurrection.

Here's the thing: we don't know if this revitalization experiment will be sustainable or not! While not-yet-Christians, brand-new Christians (lots of them), and chronologically mature Christians are all existing together in this messy blended-family scenario, we struggle financially to keep the ship afloat. This is long, slow, hard work, and God alone can make the resurrection harvest grow.

The story of Wildwood's decline is not unique. It is the new normal of US churches across the denominational spectrum. We live in a time coined "Post-Christendom," "The Great Decline," and the "Post-Christian United States." We live on a new and uncharted frontier. The land of the so-called "nones and dones" the "de-churched and the no-churched."

Unfortunately, the story of Wildwood's revitalization is unique. Most churches that decline to this level close their doors. Wildwood is not growing by Christians playing church musical chairs, or already-Christians moving their membership around. The WildOnes are among a small minority of churches across the United States growing by reaching not-yet-Christians ("professions of faith" and baptisms). In the Florida Conference, I serve in a cultivator role with hundreds of churches. Many haven't had a single baptism in years.

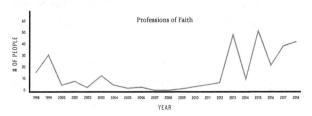

Wildwood UMC chart of "professions of faith"

Wildwood's growth may be unique, but it is not an anomaly. In fact, we are seeing something similar occur in churches across the Western missional frontier. For instance, in England, most fresh expressions are started by smaller congregations. In *Mission-shaped and Rural*, Sally Gaze observes that not only are these small rural churches cultivating fresh expressions, but the inherited congregations are taking on unexpected forms of revitalization as well.[1]

Thus, this is not just one story, this is *our* story. Or as Frederick Buechner famously said, "The story of any one of us is in some measure the story of us all." Can the spark that's happening in these churches be blown upon by the wind of the Spirit and sweep across the United States like a roaring blaze?

While the church of Jesus Christ will never die, the church as we know it is dying. You are most likely reading this book because you are convinced that this shouldn't be the case and there must be a way to revitalize existing congregations.

National director of Fresh Expressions US, Dr. Chris Backert, says there are primarily three possible paths through which a church can experience revitalization:

1. *Re-Engineering:* Looking at all the parts of a congregation's life and seeking to re-strategize, re-focus, re-organize to make the current version of the congregation its best version.

2. *Re-Vival:* That occurs through a visitation of the charismatic, a movement of the Holy Spirit that manifests in a powerful supernatural way.

3. *Re-Missioning:* By awakening and practically focusing the efforts of the congregation on the Great Commission locally. Whereas Re-Engineering starts with the "church," Re-Missioning starts with the "commission." In Re-Engineering the church sets the agenda. In Re-Missioning the mission context sets the agenda.[2]

Many of us have tried Option One more than once and we all know, even when it has been effective, the change is typically not lasting. Some would call this revitalization through church tinkering, in which we tweak what we do in the attractional model. Most books written on revitalization are focused on Option One. Doing church bigger and better: better coffee, better music, better preaching, better hospitality, and so on. This is not one of those books. Approaches that try to solve the crises facing the church from within the church are missing the point.

We are aware that Option Two is always a possibility, although we can't predict or force it to happen. Here we pray and wait. But what if the Holy Spirit is always just as active outside church walls as within them? What if God is calling us to put sneakers on our prayers and join what the Spirit is already doing in our neighborhoods and networks?

Hence, this book is an exploration of Dr. Backert's Option Three, that inherited churches can and are being revitalized by adopting the fresh expressions approach in the mixed economy or blended ecology way. While revitalization is not the goal, it is an effect of joining God's disruptive cause amid the fragmentation and isolation of human community. Cultivating fresh expressions of church births a missional ecosystem in long-declining congregations.

Revitalization is a reaction in a series of more complex chain reactions. A manifestation of *emergence*: synergistic relationships occurring between inherited and emerging modes of church that result in a new complex organism.

Let's clarify some language . . .

The Mixed Economy is a business term used to describe an economy in which some industries are privately owned and others are publicly owned or nationalized; or an economy that combines elements of capitalism and socialism. The fresh expressions movement appropriated this term to refer to a diversity of ecclesial forms in which fresh expressions of church exist alongside inherited forms in relationships of mutual respect and support.

The Blended Ecology refers to fresh expressions of church in symbiotic relationship with inherited forms of church in such a way that the combining of these attractional and missional modes blend to create a nascent form. When churches truly live into the mixed economy for an extended period, we see a transformation occur. Both the inherited church and the fresh expressions of church become a new interconnected creation . . . a blended ecology. Early in the Fresh Expressions US movement, we began to use the language of "blended ecology," which speaks more potently to the new prevalent family forms, current cultural realities, and the ancient agrarian language of Jesus' teaching.

Inherited refers to a form of church passed on as a precious gift by the saints of generations past. As in our parents leaving us an incredibly valuable inheritance that we must now learn how to steward well. Sometimes compared/

contrasted with the emerging church. Also referred to as "traditional, attractional, gathered" church.

Emerging is a contextual form of church that reaches and serves people currently outside the inherited church. They are shaped from a relational interaction between people, cultures, and the gospel. Sometimes compared/contrasted with the inherited church. Also referred to as "modern, missional, scattered," and fresh expressions of church.

A fresh expression is a form of church for our changing culture, established primarily for the benefit of those who are not yet part of any church.

Who Is This Book For?

It is frustrating to me when people write books on things they have never actually done. Don't get me wrong; we need academics writing books and formulating theories, but we also need more practitioners writing books. We need pioneers who plant their own gardens, prepare their own meals, eat their own fruits and vegetables, and share their recipes.

This book is written for local church people, by a local church person, sharing learnings from the US mission field. It is a 1 John 1:1 kind of work: "what we have heard, what we have seen with our eyes, what we have looked at and touched with our hands, concerning the word of life." We have seen the risen Jesus at work in the blended ecology way. We exchange the word *model* for *way*. As I believe the blended ecology to be a *way* for us to be the church, rather than a corporate business *model* of a new kind of church.

Denominations have tried top-down leadership strategies to reverse decline for decades; perhaps we need to give local, grassroots revolutionaries a chance. We need cohorts of local church leaders who will dig into their contexts and resist the urge to climb the corporate ladders of denominational success. In systems that often reward the politically savvy, corporate-minded ones who oil the institutional machinery and tend the company store, we need risk-taking prophets who will stand in the wilderness, thirsty among the people.

These are the strong poets who give us new language and new visions, not from the seats of power, but from the ranks of the marginalized. These are the pioneers who will stand in the liminal space and organize local people movements on a pilgrimage between the times.

If you are reading this, my hope is that you are that kind of person.

I am not writing as some expert from an ivory tower. There is no such thing as an expert on revitalization, so be careful with folks who make such claims. Only the Holy Spirit can revitalize congregations and there are countless extraneous variables in every context. However, we can adapt and reorganize existing congregations to place ourselves in the flow of the new rivers the Spirit is creating.

I have served as the pastor of several congregations that God revitalized in this way. I know the heartache of life in churches on death's doorstep. I know about trying to love people who would rather die than change. I know about the tears, frustration, and sleepless nights. The beer-bottle fight committee meetings, the betrayals, and the scars. If you know those feelings, too, this book is for you.

I am also writing as someone who is heartbroken that my own adult children identify as Christians but don't go to church. I travel the United States, sharing about the missional movement we call Fresh Expressions, hearing the stories of faithful leaders from many denominations and churches who are telling me a similar heartbreaking story: "We renovated the facilities, we hired the best music people, the most gifted youth pastor, our pastor spends fifteen hours a week preparing sermons . . . and our church is still dying."

There is hope. While the purpose of a fresh expression is *not* to revitalize existing congregations, but to reach people the church is not currently reaching, we are witnessing an interaction taking place. Churches that adopt the fresh expressions approach are being reconfigured in an inadvertent but powerful way.

The effects we can see on inherited congregations are immediately obvious: (1) they force declining congregations to awaken from apostolic amnesia, look outside themselves, and listen to their community (what I will explain in chapter 5 as breaking the toxic loop); (2) the congregation catches fire with the spirit of evangelism; (3) the "priesthood of all believers" is released as a local missionary force to offer adaptive leadership; (4) people who experience Jesus through fresh expressions sometimes matriculate back to the existing congregation; and (5) the church reorganizes itself around the new disruptive work of the Spirit taking place.

I believe God can and will revitalize churches, but it often occurs through a fundamental recalibration of local congregations. In part 2, I will propose four moves to describe the process of revitalization: *awakening, futurefitting, cultivating/grafting*, and *releasing*. Each of these moves is broken down into a chapter. I believe the process enables every existing congregation, no matter the size, to become in a sense a multi-site. Inherited churches can launch fresh expressions, harnessing the power of resurrection already in their midst.

Cultivating, Seeding, and Grafting

Let us enter the ecosystem of scriptural imagination with three Jesus stories we must hold together in tension.

The Parable of the Barren Fig Tree

> Then he told this parable: "A man had a fig tree planted in his vineyard; and he came looking for fruit on it and found none. So he said

to the gardener, 'See here! For three years I have come looking for fruit on this fig tree, and still I find none. Cut it down! Why should it be wasting the soil?' He replied, 'Sir, let it alone for one more year, until I dig around it and put manure on it. If it bears fruit next year, well and good; but if not, you can cut it down.'" (Luke 13:6–9)

Overall, this is a story of God's patient and persistent love. After being challenged consistently by the religious leadership of his day, Jesus is responding with a story about the barrenness of those leaders and the bankrupt nature of the religious system.

If we see the owner of the field as God, then we understand that God expects trees to bear fruit. We can understand the frustration of the vineyard owner. Here is a tree wasting the space and nutrients of the soil. If we understand Jesus as the gardener, we see his compassionate heart to provide some TLC that will nurse the tree back to health. He gets down on his hands and knees to do the dirty work of fertilization and cultivation. Perhaps the three years are the three years of Jesus' ministry.

We can make some easy connections here to our own context. Jesus gets down on his hands and knees to cultivate new life in people and systems. Speaking of local churches, there are many that appear at times to be wasting the soil of their communities—occupying space but bearing little fruit in the lives of people. The good news is that Jesus doesn't give up on us. No one likes to be dug up, pruned, or covered in manure, but the transformation process from barrenness to fruitfulness is never easy.

It is the desire of Jesus that all churches should bear fruit, and he is with us, down on his knees doing the dirty work of tilling, pruning, and fertilizing. Just as in the incarnation, he gets dirt beneath his fingernails so the church is called to this work of revitalizing barren trees.

The Parable of the Sower

> *"Listen! A sower went out to sow. And as he sowed, some seeds fell on the path, and the birds came and ate them up. Other seeds fell on rocky ground, where they did not have much soil, and they sprang up quickly, since they had no depth of soil. But when the sun rose, they were scorched; and since they had no root, they withered away. Other seeds fell among thorns, and the thorns grew up and choked them. Other seeds fell on good soil and brought forth grain, some a hundredfold, some sixty, some thirty. Let anyone with ears listen!"*
> (Matt. 13:3–9)

The parable of the sower is a story about the profuse, generative love of God. The sower casts the seed far and wide, generously across the landscape. The seed doesn't change; every seed has the potential for new life. The goal of the sower is to produce a crop. The potential of the seed can be limited by the condition of the soil; seeds can't grow to fruition in rocky, shallow, or crowded soil.

The church is called to profusely and generatively cast the seeds of God's love into the world.

In the blended ecology, both the work of the gardener tilling, pruning, and fertilizing existing trees so that they might bear fruit, and the sower going out to cast the seeds that will one day yield a harvest are equally important. We must do the work of stewarding and caring for the inherited church, that it may produce much fruit. We must hold that work in creative tension with being sent to cast the seeds on the new missional frontier—planting the emerging forms of church, offering God's love to those who will receive it in fresh ways.

The Parable of the Vine

"I am the true vine, and my Father is the vinegrower. He removes every branch in me that bears no fruit. Every branch that bears fruit he prunes to make it bear more fruit. You have already been cleansed by the word that I have spoken to you. Abide in me as I abide in you. Just as the branch cannot bear fruit by itself unless it abides in the vine, neither can you unless you abide in me. I am the vine, you are the branches. Those who abide in me and I in them bear much fruit, because apart from me you can do nothing. Whoever does not abide in me is thrown away like a branch and

withers; such branches are gathered, thrown into the fire, and burned." (John 15: 1–6)

In this parable, Jesus himself is the living organism, the *true vine*, his living essence flows through the whole complex network of the vineyard. The father is the vinegrower. God himself is doing the work of pruning, fertilizing, and removing the parts that do not bear fruit. Once again, the focus of Jesus' agrarian metaphors is the expectation of fruit-bearing. Who's doing all the work in this analogy? God! We are the branches; our only function is to abide. Abiding in Christ, our being with him, results in bearing fruit for him. We are all part of the same vineyard, all connected, by Jesus himself.

The blended ecology requires a third move: grafting.

The grafting process involves combining a shoot system (called a scion) of one species with the root system (called a rootstock) of another. There is an exchange at a fundamental level in which the two species not only enter a symbiotic union, but they transform each other. A new kind of grape is created from the union—a new creation. This is the understanding of revitalization I will seek to explore.

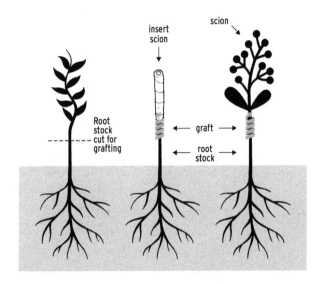

The vineyard is a place of deep roots *and* wild branches. It is a complex, interweaving, organic, polycentric, dispersed, networked system. What if local congregations were to base themselves, structurally speaking, on Jesus' parable of the vine, rather than some corporate entity?

We will hold these three images—cultivating, seeding, and grafting—together throughout the book.

CHAPTER 1
The Desert

We are in a Judges 2:10 situation, "Moreover, that whole generation was gathered to their ancestors, and *another generation grew up* after them, *who did not know the* LORD *or the work that he had done for Israel*" (italics mine).

How is it that one God-following generation can endure the wilderness wandering, cross into the promised land, and then fail epically to pass the faith on to the next generation? It happened in Judges 2, and it's happened again in the twenty-first-century United States. As Mark Twain is reported to have quipped, "History doesn't repeat itself, but it does rhyme."

The inherited church was planted in a different ecosystem. Let's just say it was like a jungle, a wild untamed frontier bursting with all kinds of life-forms and many diverse challenges. The ecosystem changed, like a desert that swallowed up the jungle. The church in the United States has been through a series of seismic sandstorms. Our instinctual response has been to hunker down in the walls of our churches, hoping the storms will soon pass. Before we knew it, we were buried in the sands of a new desert ecosystem.

While certainly different than a jungle, a desert is also an ecosystem. An ecosystem is simply a community of living organisms, interacting with each other in a physical environment. A desert ecosystem is typically characterized by little to no precipitation or water sources. Deserts are usually arid, with sparse vegetation and extreme temperatures. However, deserts are not devoid of life; they just have different varieties of life. Think of the various species of plants, mammals, reptiles, insects, and birds that call the desert home. Living things adapt to their ecosystem.

The church is in a new ecosystem, and we have failed to adapt.

The twenty-first century has been a time of seismic shifts. While all the world has changed around us, the church has remained largely fixed in our response to the emerging missional opportunity. While the world has been moving at blazing 5G speeds, we have been stuck on rotary telephones.

Changing Landscape—Post-Everything

I want to now provide six sketches of the major shifts that have contributed to the decline of Christianity in the United States. The multiplicity and speed of change is pushing us into a post-everything age. Much more could be said here.

The six shifts are not meant as an exhaustive list, and I share them in appetizer-sized bites.

1. *Economy:* From Dead Presidents to Bitcoin

We are in a time of incredible economic change. The housing market crash, persistently high unemployment, a rise in wealth for the privileged minority, income inequality for the masses, and stagnation in standard-of-living growth are the persistent North American hardships of recent years. The economic dilemma of this emerging generation is created by a convergence of unemployment, globalization, automation, foreign competition, a faltering education system, and massive educational debt.[1] The postindustrial digital age has dawned. With this globalized and knowledge-based economy as the new financial reality, there is a growing chasm between the super wealthy and everyone else. The massive unbalanced distribution of wealth has diminished the existence of the middle class that was once the primary volunteer base of churches—what Paul Taylor calls "a hollowing of the middle."[2] Members no longer enjoy relatively steady nine-to-five jobs, pension plans, paid vacations, and weekends off. The new US economic landscape is a 24/7 work culture. Many people now work on weekends.

Bitcoin illustrates this shift. Globalized civilization is moving toward redefining and potentially abolishing the center of all current economic systems . . . money itself.

In our lifetime, we may see the decentralization of minted currency. Bitcoin was the first attempt at a decentralized, distributed currency that needed no central bank. It is a shared, networked system of currency powered by a mathematical technology called "blockchain." This radical technology has the capacity to decentralize most systems. While some see Bitcoin as a failed attempt (it was immediately harnessed and used illegally in the trafficking of narcotics), blockchain has planted the seeds of a disruptive innovation that may be the future of a globalized economy.

2. Family: From Beaver, to Brady Bunch, to Modern Family

While using the term *post-family* would be going too far, "post-familialism" is an accurate description of today's reality to which the church must adapt.[3] Even the need to have a family in the sense of settling down and having children is something undergoing transformation.

Just consider the evolution of the sitcoms or situational comedies that have portrayed family life being broadcasted into US homes for seventy years. *Leave It to Beaver* is almost beyond generational memory now, but it captured the 1950's ideal nuclear family structure (i.e., two parents; a man and a woman; usually two children). By the 1970s *The Brady Bunch* burst onto the scene, in some ways ahead of its time, but reflective of the newly emerging reality of remixed familial structures. Carol and Michael Brady bring their families together with six children (three boys and three girls), a dog, and their housekeeper, Alice. While the blended family unit was somewhat of an emergent improvisation then, this is no longer the case.

In 2010, *Modern Family* was released. This family is complete with adoptions, multiple habitation, straight, gay, multicultural, and blended traditional. This is an accurate reflection of the change in familial dynamics to date. The blended family, where parents bring children together from previous relationships, and the single-parent family, have been growing steadily as the dominant family forms in the United States.

The definition, structure, and societal expectations of family have changed. *The Mission-shaped Church* report notes several shifts that translate across Western society: rises in divorce, single parents, stepfamilies, adults who decide not to have children, cohabitating couples, and single persons, all contribute to the decline of the inherited church.[4] One practical implication for the church is the reality of visitation in these new parental arrangements, where non-custodial parents rotate weekends.

For the most part, the church continues to function, structure, and program toward the *Leave It to Beaver* days. Our systems are designed for the nuclear family model. Essentially, we have not even gone *Brady Bunch* yet, much less *Modern Family*!

3. Religion: From Christendom to Pantheon

While the population is growing, church attendance is declining. Furthermore, studies indicate that people report going to church more than they really do. Robert Putnam notes that careful survey comparisons reveal that parishioners "misremember" whether they attended services, overreporting attendance by as much as 50 percent.[5]

The "nones" are the fastest-growing group (those that report no religious affiliation). The perspective of those with a growing tendency of disaffiliation is interesting. Certain myths are perpetuated about this group that are not exactly accurate. A 2012 survey offers some insight. Of the 46 million unaffiliated adults, 68 percent believe in God. Thirty-seven percent self-describe as "spiritual but not religious," and 1 in 5 reportedly pray every day (21 percent).[6] They are not anti-Jesus, just anti-church.

Perhaps we are seeing the emergence of a new nonconformist movement. People are open and even hungry for spiritual meaning, but the common assumption is that it cannot be found in institutional religion. The emerging spirituality is once again "protest-ant," protesting and pushing against the established hierarchies.

Within the living memory of some North Americans is the time of the "Blue Laws," those restrictions designed to ban Sunday activities to promote the observance of a day of Sabbath. The time of Blue Laws is over. The age of the new pantheon has come. The Roman pantheon syncretized worship to include the noteworthy gods from subjugated peoples. In the syncretistic new pantheonic thinking, all the gods share the same mythical space. They are equally able to meet spiritual hunger and add value to our lives. Most Christians in the United States now report that "many religions lead to eternal life."[7]

4. Technology: From Morse Code to Virtual Reality

Technology is not only changing every industry, it is changing society and the meaning of community itself. Look at the history of broadcasting for instance. Morse code (the wireless telegraph) burst onto the scene in the late 1890s. Commercial radio broadcasting was emerging in the 1920s. In 1939, theater audiences were dazzled by *The Wizard of Oz* as Dorothy walked into Technicolor and realized she wasn't in Kansas anymore. Up until the 1950s most US families rallied around a radio for weekly broadcasts. By the 1960s color televisions were becoming widely available. Since that time, Americans have gathered around their televisions to get their news from the three national broadcasting networks: CBS, NBC, and ABC. New technologies have transformed all of this. Millennials, the first "digital natives," now use social media to receive and disseminate news.

Through the various livestream features you can experience momentous events as they unfold. Televisions themselves will become obsolete. Now, experimental technologies in virtual reality are not simply providing a one-dimensional optical and aural experience, but full sensory immersion. In the 1970s the clunky personal computer was beginning to become available; today we carry around miniature supercomputers on our wrists or in our pockets.

Tech-driven, knowledge-based systems are helping eliminate extreme poverty, increase mobility, and allow mass access to decentralized education. Mobility is allowing longer commutes, pursuit of jobs, and decreased loyalty to a central space where we would live and work our entire lives. What are the implications of these technological revolutions for the church? Why would a newcomer wake up early, on their only day off, and drive to a church for a highly contextual message for a group of strangers? There is no shortage of inspiring messages available at the command of our voice; it only takes two words: "Hey, Siri." In seconds, a plethora of sermons pop up by professional, polished speakers, not contextually confined to local parishes. Consider the banquet of TED Talks alone, which can be deeply spiritual, may even be equally transformative, not as long, and with no plea for money in the end!

5. Neighborhood: From *Mister Rogers' Neighborhood* to Neo's *Matrix*

All these shifts contribute to this sketch. Community itself has been remixed. There has been a significant erosion of social capital and the concept of neighboring.

I was one of the millions of children impacted by the incredible life of Fred Rogers. From 1968, on and off to 2001, *Mister Rogers' Neighborhood* was a steady force for positively shaping the development of children. Live on public television, Fred Rodgers subversively taught generations about the importance of learning, the values of neighborly kindness, and compassion.

Mister Rogers' Neighborhood is no more—neither the show nor the potentiality it envisioned. We have moved from Fred Rogers' neighborhood into the fictional computer hacker character Neo's *Matrix*.

The *Matrix* films are prophetic in the sense that the kind of fictional community we see there is becoming reality. Beside the urbanization and clustered-but-isolated living arrangements of Neo's pre-red-pill world, the films also capture the sense of people living in two worlds, both the actual and the digital. One is about creating avatars and escaping into a virtual realm, the other is the random daily encounters that happen between the screens we now live our lives on. Television screens, phone screens, work computer screens, dashboard screens, and so on.

In this new matrix of networks, the makeup of neighborhoods themselves are undergoing a major remix. New smaller households are growing faster than the population, due to the familial shifts described earlier. As the population grows, urbanization and the increasing lack of space is creating smaller self-contained, dormitory-like structures. In the network scenario, *neighborhoods* become secondary to *flows* of communication, information, and mobility, enabled by technology. People gather across geographic boundaries around shared *practices* that predominately take place in neutral *third places*. This shift was captured in *The Mission-shaped Church* report, "The Western world, at the start of the third millennium, is best described as a 'network society.' This is a fundamental change: 'the emergence of a new social order.'"[8]

Here we can lean into the pioneering work of sociologist Manuel Castells, who describes this new societal order in depth. Within this post-industrial, knowledge-based era now described as the Information age, technology has made the world smaller. Humanity is now a truly global community. Microelectronic and communication technologies serve as flows that enable us to connect across geographies and time. The new organization of this global community is a complex series of interconnected networks. Castells posits that at the end of the second millennium, a new form of society arose from the interactions of several major social, technological, economic, and cultural transformations.

Network Society consists of a social structure made up of networks enabled by micro-electronics-based information and communications technologies.[9]

The emerging societal structure is constructed around technologically enabled flows of capital, information, organizational interaction, images, sounds, and symbols. The *flows* refer to the means of social organization, the expression of processes dominating our economic, political, and symbolic life.[10] Thus, in a network society, culture is now mobile, moving along a complex web of interconnected networks; flows are about the movement of people, objects, and things from one node to another in social space. Cultures consist of bundles of dynamic practices, connected across space and time through structured flows of information and media. *Practices* are simply the activities carried out or performed by a group of people habitually or regularly in these social spaces. Flows are the means through which these movements and connections occur.[11]

The church is seemingly still stuck in the Fred Rogers' neighborhood model, while existing in a *Matrix* world of networks connected by flows.

6. *Church:* From Constantine, to North American Imperial Cult, Back to Caves

The final shift is within the church itself. The dominant North American version of church goes back to

Emperor Constantine in AD 313 when Christianity became the state religion. Up until then, Christians were a rogue—and periodically illegal—religious movement that experienced several rounds of imperial persecution. At times, the primitive church met in secret spaces, subversively scratching the fish symbol (*Ichthys*) on cave walls to identify meeting places. This small renegade movement, with little resources, no buildings, no professional clergy, and no committee meetings, between the time of Jesus' death on the cross in the 30s and Constantine in the 300s, grew numerically across vast geographical distances. They became a force to be reckoned with.

The blending of religion and state power had both positive and negative effects. Not being arrested, punished, or having your property confiscated was certainly a plus. The days of meeting secretly in caves and catacombs was largely over. Yet, adversely, vast church building projects were launched of unparalleled grandeur. No longer a minority, many good citizens became Christian. This created a need for professional full-time priests to care for the growing masses. This is the attractional model: *build it and they will come.*

The United States has operated in the Christendom assumption that we are a Christian nation and that the church enjoys a central role in Western culture. Protestant denominations adopted the organizational structure of the twentieth-century corporation and benefited greatly for a season. However, emerging generations are not buying this amalgamation of Christ and empire.

We have built it, and they have not come. More Americans now hold a secular worldview than a Christian one. The Christendom model as we know it, our dominant Western version of the faith, is disintegrating.

Picnic Talk

Reminder—Creating a Habitat of Listening

Scripture Focus: Read Judges 2:10

1. Discuss what impressions you have from reading Judges 2:10. Do you see a parallel with the North American context?

2. Why do you think emerging generations are resistant to the church? Did the generational breakdown start in the home, the church, or both?

3. Has the church done a good job producing disciples of Jesus Christ? Why or why not?

4. Do you find the language of different ecosystems helpful in understanding how the North American landscape has changed? In what ways would you describe our current mission field as a desert?

5. Do you see these six shifts contributing to the decline of Christianity? If so, how have you seen them influencing your church? In what ways?

6. Do your children and/or grandchildren attend church regularly? Why or why not?

CHAPTER 2

Resurrection—The Power Transforming Ecosystems

God turns deserts into jungles. God turns cemeteries into gardens. God makes dead things come alive again. We describe the power God uses to do this with the word *resurrection*.

How exactly does God make one a new creation in the present? It's certainly not that God throws us into a dumpster and starts over. God works with the existing material, reshaping and recreating. God's way of "making all things new" (Rev. 21:5) is not our consumeristic way of brand-spanking newness and waste. It's the way of potters remixing at wheels and shattered lives reassembling in new amalgamations.

The formational story of the Christian faith is the resurrection of Jesus Christ from the dead. Resurrection is the ultimate narrative of disruption. The empty tomb throws a monkey wrench in the death-dealing cycle of business as usual. It changes everything. Resurrection is the power that dismantles all other forms of power.

Without the resurrection of Jesus from the dead, Paul reminds us, we are without hope and pathetic (1 Cor. 15:17–19). Jesus is the "firstfruits" of the resurrection (1 Cor. 15:20–28), his risen enfleshed self is the prototype, so to speak, of what all humanity ultimately is in the process of becoming. The ultimate plan for the entire cosmos is resurrection. In Romans, Paul describes the universe as shuttering in the throes of birth pangs, like a woman bared down delivering a child; the broken creation is trembling with the force of new creation by the power of resurrection (Rom. 8:19–23).

Resurrection is a force of remix, a power that transforms death and decay and infuses it with new life. It is the way of the triune God, it demonstrates the graceful heart of a Creator who refuses to waste anyone or anything. God's answer to dilapidation is renovation. God's answer to sin-broken creation is a new creation. God's answer to isolation is communion. God's answer to fallen lives is restoration and renewal. God's answer to polluted ecosystems is a process of healing that brings streams in the deserts, repopulation of forests in barren wastelands, and flowing waters from a restored temple. God's answer to death is resurrection.

God's answer to decline is revitalization. The God who "[makes] all things new" (Rev. 21:5) is always doing new things. Always making the withered trees flourish again. Across the United States and beyond, God is up to something. In the cracks of the concrete jungle of our post-everything world, new wild seedlings are pushing through and unfurling in a wonderful tapestry of life. Across a Christian landscape that looks and feels like a desert of decline, new oases of life are springing forth.

Dry trees are coming back to life, standing firm in all their elegant, shade-offering glory. Organic communities of innovation are forming people networks across the shifting landscape.

The fullest resurrection image we have in Scripture is found in Revelation 22. There we find a remixed urban-garden scenario centered around the tree. The last time humanity saw the tree of life was during our forceful expulsion from Eden after the epic failure of sin, the fall, and death. Yet the ultimate vision of hope we glimpse here is a return-from-exile kind of hope. There we find ourselves in a glorious new ecosystem. Not as disembodied spirits floating on pillowy clouds playing harps, but in a very real, embodied scenario, back in the very much real garden. A New Jerusalem descends from the heavens.

This garden is a remix. It has some of the elements of Eden; the tree is there, God is there, the river is there, and we are there. But now it is an urban garden. There in the city is the tree.

> Then the angel showed me the river of the water of life, as clear as crystal, flowing from the throne of God and of the Lamb down the middle of the great street of the city. On each side of the river stood the tree of life, bearing twelve crops of fruit, yielding its fruit every month. And the leaves of the tree are for the healing of the nations. (Rev. 22:1–2 NIV)

Today, cities are already becoming urban gardens, with green spaces that invite communion and play, where our isolation can be healed.

Unfortunately, it is our human nature to always focus on the vastness of the desert, rather than the little generative ecosystems dotting the landscape. Yet if we were to turn our attention to those microenvironments and seek to understand them, we could potentially multiply what is taking place. If some trees can flourish and take on new dimensions of life, there is at least a chance others can as well. If the Spirit is moving there, disrupting the cycles of waterless decline, can we deduce the Spirit desires to manifest that disruptive work in other places?

The mega metaphor of this book is the central image of deeply rooted desert trees bursting with wild cascades of life and replicating everywhere. The trees, the *inherited* churches, are giving and receiving life from *emerging* forms of life, the fresh expressions. This symbiotic relationship is possible in most contexts and is already starting to happen across the missional frontier.

Quite simply, the resurrection power of Jesus operating through inherited forms of church + emerging forms of church = the emergence of a greater whole some would identify as revitalization.

Just as resurrection is a remix of existing materials, so when the attractional and missional forms of church are blended together they create the blended ecology.

If we believe God has the power to make all things new, why do we doubt that God has the power to revitalize dying churches? Is that too big a task for this God of resurrection? Yet the very strategies of denominations and church networks expose their doubt in the central defining narrative of Jesus. The common lingo around church revitalization is sometimes, "It's easier to give birth than to raise the dead." However, that's not exactly true. Just ask any woman who has ever given birth how easy it was. For God, it is *not* easier to give birth than to raise the dead; God is quite competent at both. Yes, we need to plant new churches (giving birth), *and* we need to revitalize existing churches (revitalization), both by the power of the Spirit.

In the blended ecology, we can give birth and raise the dead at the same time. Our proclivity to give birth rather than raise the dead is indicative of a deeper problem. We have domesticated our understanding of the power of resurrection. Church vitality "experts" spend more time talking through corporate diagrams of church life cycles than telling the stories of the widow of Nain's son, Jairus's daughter, Lazarus, Tabitha, Eutychus, or Jesus. The "disembodied souls floating into the cloud" kind of theology leads to a disembodied faith; a faith that no longer sees very embodied, real people in the pews of existing churches as valuable. Congregations that have been outposts of the kingdom of God for many decades become disposable. The valuable properties they have amassed equate to big dollars that can be spent on planting new churches.

In the words of Dr. Phil, "How's that working for you?" We've been journeying down that road for some time now, so where is the fruit? This strategy is now being realized as futile. *The Mission-shaped Church* team identifies church planting as a "supplementary strategy." They say, "Perhaps the most significant recommendation of this current report is that this is no longer adequate."[1] Planting new churches will not stem the tide of decline. Both planting new churches and revitalizing existing ones is the way forward . . . doing both together in existing congregations is the blended ecology way.

Your Church Needs to Die

"Very truly, I tell you, unless a grain of wheat falls into the earth and dies, it remains just a single grain; but if it dies, it bears much fruit" (John 12:24).

Much of Jesus' teaching was wrapped in the agricultural stories of his context. Our language of fresh expressions and blended ecologies, new life and resurrection, all starts with a seed. This truth is often overlooked. A seed that is never placed in the ground never bears fruit. The same focus of the gardener, the sower, and the vinedresser is to eventually bear fruit. This is language of the harvest. The people who follow Jesus are people of seeds, vines, trees, and harvests.

Your church doesn't need to *close*; it needs to *die*. We need to die in the same sense that Jesus describes here. When we are willing to go into the ground, die to our current form, and yield to the power of resurrection, we can emerge fully alive for a new season of harvest. The problem is that most churches are not willing to die. Like someone with a terminal diagnosis, we can get caught in a toxic loop of denial. Rather than yielding to the care of potential treatment, we deny the condition and die a slow and painful death.

The church is not in the self-preservation business, the church is in the self-donation business. The very eucharistic nature of the body of Christ is to break pieces of ourselves off and give them away to a hungry world. Unfortunately, when our church is caught in a decline cycle, we clench our fists, desperately grasping at what's left. Yet, if we open our hands and give what we are away through our own self-death, we release God to catalyze resurrection.

Denominational and local church strategies focused on preserving the institution have it backward. Our way forward is a journey of death and resurrection, not more institutional solutions to institutional problems. Fresh Expressions is not another "church revitalization strategy" or "save the denomination plan" but a die-and-give-ourselves-away plan. The blended ecology allows local churches to break pieces of themselves off and give them away by planting fresh expressions in their communities. We, in a sense, die so that we can truly live as a new creation.

The power of Jesus that broke the grave also transforms ecosystems and revitalizes churches.

Picnic Talk

Scripture Focus: Read John 12:24

1. Discuss what impressions you have after reading John 12:24. How does this passage speak to you about revitalization?

2. What do you believe are the main reasons why thousands of churches close every year? How do you think God feels about this?

3. Do you agree that church planting alone is not a viable mission strategy for the US context? Why or why not?

4. How do you understand the power of resurrection? In what ways do you see it at work in the world now?

5. Do you agree that giving birth and raising the dead are equally possible for God?

6. Do you believe your church can be revitalized? Why or why not?

7. In what ways do you believe your church needs to die to experience resurrection? What things need to go into the ground so a new creation can emerge?

CHAPTER 3

Fresh Expressions— Wild Branches

It's approaching noonish on a Saturday morning. A group of almost thirty people are circling up in a green space, in this case, a local dog park. They make small talk about their dogs as they watch them run and play. Some take selfies, groupies, and/or catch pictures and clips of their dogs doing funny stuff. As random folks show up to unleash their dogs, some of the more outgoing members strike up conversations. "What kind of dog is that?" "What's your dog's name?" and so on. The children run, play, fall, climb trees, and enjoy getting a little muddy beneath the canopy of mighty oaks.

An older gentleman wearing a Miami Hurricanes hat suddenly calls the group together to start the church service, but not with those words. Yes, this is a church service! It's a fresh expression of church called Paws of Praise meeting in a dog park. Churchish things are happening, they just look a little different. Something can't really be called church unless stepping in crap is a real possibility, right?

As the humans have their "passing of the peace," hugging, pounding, and selfie-ing, the dogs are having their own version, a "sniffing of the butts," if you will. Rather than signing an attendance pad, many check in on their various social media accounts—the technology that connected them here. There is no choir, organ, or praise band, but nature provides a wonderful orchestra of birds and other animals, whose rhythms of being offer their own kind of hymnic praise to God. Relationships are being formed, connections made, even a little gossip here and there.

Most of those gathered are middle-aged or younger, but not everyone. Many of the ladies are wearing yoga pants, running gear, shorts, and other Florida-appropriate attire. The guys are dressed the same, minus the yoga pants. Not exactly Sunday-best suits and ties, but closer to how Jesus and his disciples probably dressed as they traveled the roads together.

The older gentleman with the bad taste in hats—we will just call him Larry—has no credentials, no seminary education, nor professional ministry position within any church, but he is the pastor of this church. As the spiritual leader of this community, he offers a brief devotional. As if the dogs know the churchy part has begun, many come and sit with their masters, taking a break from the slobbery melee to listen and rest.

Spiritually speaking, the group is a strange amalgamation of folks. A few are mature Christians, some are brand-new Christians, others are surely not Christian. Some are good people, who were hurt by bad Christians. Some are bad people becoming good Christians. A couple of visitors were invited by friends or saw the gathering in Meetup.com or Facebook. Some were just taking their dogs for a walk but were curiously drawn to the gathering. They fill the benches and break out lawn chairs. Some take out the super-computers in their pockets and read the Scripture Larry is explaining, others just listen.

When Larry is done, he prompts questions and people begin to share. Some speak of profound struggles they had last week. One celebrates that she got a job, and thanks the group for prayers. One young lady shares that she thinks God spoke to her for the first time last week. One young man reports that his girlfriend broke up with him and he's bummed.

In this space, newcomers ask great questions like, "So Jesus is actually God?" They pray out loud before a group for the first time. They confess getting wasted and how they think they might be struggling with that. Some will take Communion for the first time. Many will come back.

Some call this gathering their church. Others will show up to check out what the Sunday thing is all about.

This is just one fresh expression within a larger network of fresh expressions in Wildwood, Florida. Just about every day of the week, one of these gatherings is taking place at various times. Other fresh expressions meet in the local Mexican restaurant, Burritos and Bibles. One meets in a tattoo parlor, Tattoo Parlor Church. One called Connect meets in the Martin Luther King Jr. building. Another meets in a makeshift yoga studio called Yoga Therapy Church. Church 3.1 is a group who gather in a park, then do church on the run . . . literally (a 5k, to be exact.)

One, a group for single women seeking to be sanctified, called Mascara Mondays, meets in a coffee shop. Another meets in a beautician's shop called Shear Love at Soul Salon. These are just a few fresh expressions of a single church. None of them cost anything, but some of them send money back to the inherited church.

People are connecting with God in each of these groups at different levels in different ways. The likelihood that any one of them would have ever darkened the door of a church compound on a Sunday morning is little to none.

Yet here they are, having church in the spaces and places where they do life every day, connected by the flows of a network society, sharing in communal practices. They are little communities of Jesus, scattered throughout the communal ecosystem like green spaces.

Green Space refers to the little islands of vegetation in predominantly urban environments. These are places featuring grass, shrubs, trees, and other vegetation dedicated to encouraging play, connection, and pause.

For our purposes, green spaces are the first, second, and third places where people do life. This "place" language comes from the foundational work of sociologist Ray Oldenburg.

First Place: The home or primary place of residence.

Second Place: The workplace or school place.

Third Place: The public places separate from the two usual social environments of home and workplace, that "host regular, voluntary, informal, and happily anticipated gatherings of individuals." Some examples are environments such as cafes, pubs, clubs, parks, and so on.[1]

Urban environmentalism is growing popular with tremendous speed. We are amid a paradigm shift that will shape the future of cities and the planet. By adapting an integrated approach that includes economic, social, and environmental aspects into urban design, cities are being reconsidered in how they relate to the greater ecosystem on which all life depends. Most of these projects seem to follow two major patterns: strategies to retrofit existing cities with green technology, and entire cities designed from the start for sustainability and low environmental impact, powered by renewable energy. Masdar City, literally a desert settlement of Abu Dhabi, in the United Arab Emirates is one of the latter.[2]

Learning how to build sustainable cities in a desert is great; however, in many parts of the United States and Europe, the critical challenge leans more toward dealing with aging building materials and unsustainable urban infrastructure. Across the United States, a new breed of urban engineers is employing imagination, creativity, and innovative technologies to retrofit existing cities. They are discovering that, through retrofitting, the potential of cities may also provide their solutions.

Retrofitting existing cities is the greatest task to healing our ecosystem and enabling human thriving in the future. We need some of our best and brightest minds working on the remixing of neighborhoods in a sustainable way and creating green space.

The church is facing a similar challenge today. Rather than retrofitting cities for sustainability, we need to be futurefitting inherited congregations for revitalization. While we need to continue with Masdar City–like church plants, we need to make futurefitting existing congregations for sustainability our most pressing work.

Futurefitting is different than retrofitting. Retrofitting refers to the addition of new technology or features to older systems. In urban planning, engineers are tasked with retrofitting cities to minimize pollution and improve the quality of life. Futurefitting refers to the planting of fresh expressions in communal ecosystems and restructuring inherited congregations in the blended ecology way to create a sustainable future. Futurefitting is a more appropriate description of the Spirit's work of cultivating wild colonies of new creation in existing communities. Remember, giving birth and raising the dead are equally reflective of the triune God.

God is futurefitting communities now with the life of heaven to come.

In a world that is beginning to design eco-cities, it's time for us to design some eco-churches. If we want to see our churches become everything God has called them to be, we must stop thinking from within the paradigm of church revitalization. We need to think of the task before us as cultivating a new communal ecosystem, complete with green technology. The hard reality is that your church may still die in the process, but it can plant the seeds of its DNA in the soils of a new future.

The church plays a significant role in the complex networks within the ecosystem. It is like a green space within that network. It provides the life-giving oxygen that helps the community breathe and heal from isolation. It is a haven, an oasis for the 24/7 work-anxiety cycle of our world. In most cases, the people in our communities have become habituated to living in the unsustainable cycles of pollution and sin. They are largely unaware of the need to recreate the community in a sustainable way, so we will need to open the imaginations of our community to this reality.

Resurrection by futurefit must become the new normal of the inherited church. How do we allow the Holy Spirit to blow a breath of fresh air on our inherited congregations, while at the same time harnessing imagination, innovation, and disruption to birth nascent faith communities? In the blended ecology, every local church has the capacity to plant new churches. Every minister becomes a church planter of sorts. Every clergy person becomes a mini-bishop in the larger ecosystem.

Fresh Expressions—A Breath of Fresh Air

The preface to the Declaration of Assent says,

> The Church of England is part of the One, Holy, Catholic and Apostolic Church, worshiping the one true God, Father, Son and Holy Spirit. It professes the faith uniquely revealed in the Holy Scriptures and set forth in the catholic creeds,

which faith the Church is called upon to proclaim afresh in each generation (italics mine).[3]

It is the conviction of this statement, captured by the *Mission-shaped Church* team, from which Fresh Expressions was identified in 2004. Fresh Expressions is a movement of the Holy Spirit cultivating new forms of church alongside existing congregations to reach a changing world. The focus is doing life alongside not-yet-Christians as we are formed as disciples of Jesus Christ together. As we Fresh Expressions US people say, it's about "reaching new people, in new places, in new ways." The folks of the United Kingdom are from our future. They are out ahead of the United States in the great decline of Christianity. They are now out ahead of the United States once again, leading the way on the new missional frontier.

The Fresh Expressions movement, born in the United Kingdom, has jumped over to the United States and taken on a life of its own. Just in the Florida Conference of the UMC alone, we have seen almost two hundred of these communities emerge in the last couple of years, most of them tethered to inherited congregations. Furthermore, there are multiple similar movements using different terminology like "witnessing communities" and "missional communities" that are being the church where life happens, such as Forge International, 3DM, or Church

Multiplication Association. Beyond the "global north," these communities are cropping up in Barbados, Chile, South Africa, and elsewhere.[4]

By the way, just so you are aware, it's not really that fresh either; it's as old as the church itself. If there has been a church of Jesus Christ, a Spirit-filled, equipped, and sent community, that church has always been expressing itself in fresh, incarnational, relational, contextual, and missional ways. If you add two words to "fresh expressions" you can really wrap your head around it: "fresh expressions *of church*." Fresh expressions are simply that— new, creative manifestations of the one, holy, catholic, and apostolic church of Jesus Christ. These fresh expressions just might not look like our grandmother's church. They are the wild branches, springing up all around the missional ecosystem.

Let's take a look at how one formed in the book of Acts. Indeed, the church of Jesus Christ is a fresh expression of Judaism, so to speak. But also, already in the very genesis of the movement, fresh expressions are emerging from the church.

Look at Acts 16:6–15, where we can see a primary example of how fresh expressions of church happen. Notice here the language of the Spirit guiding, directing, stopping, and communicating through visions. Paul's work on the missional frontier is not led by him, but by the Holy Spirit. Also notice the language of the Holy Spirit and the Spirit of Jesus used almost interchangeably. As we plant the seeds of the gospel among strange communal ecosystems, we are never doing so alone. We are following Jesus, keeping pace with what the Holy Spirit is already doing in the world. So much of what we do in the Fresh Expressions movement is all about listening.

Paul's typical custom was to start at the synagogue (Acts 17:2). It was his missional practice to start with the inherited community. However, in Philippi, a leading Roman colony, there was apparently no synagogue presence. I think there is a lesson in Paul's activity about always starting with the local church when there is one available. Christianity as a fresh expression itself starts in the temple and local synagogues. There is much work of renewal and freshening up to do there.

Paul and company then heard about a place of prayer down by the river. (Notice Paul was not a heroic solo leader; they were working together as a team. Luke wrote from a firsthand perspective.) This was a gathering of people in the green spaces, spiritually open, centered around the practice of prayer in whatever form that practice took. Paul worked at the inherited stations, but also knew how to find the gatherings of people doing life together connecting around practices through flows (in his day, the complex system of Roman highways). It was there he could often seed the gospel in alien cultures.

The group at this place of prayer looked very different than the synagogue crowd. They were women, for one! Furthermore, one of these women was not typical in the patriarchal Jewish culture of the day. She was a kind of CEO of her own corporation, dealing in purple cloth. As purple cloth was reserved for royalty and the wealthy, we can assume Lydia was a person of significant means.

Her entire household was baptized, and she offered for Paul and team to come stay in "my home," another sign of her significant wealth.

The emphasis is not on Paul's forceful oratory, but that the "Lord opened her heart" (Acts 16:14). Jesus is always with us on the missional frontier; we are merely collaborating with his efforts. Even when simply praying the Lord's Prayer in a public venue, we never know what hearts the Lord may be opening.

The first church at Philippi was a fresh expression meeting at Lydia's house. It started in a third place, then moved to a first place. Lydia was what Jesus described in the missional blueprint in Luke 10 as a "person of peace." (We will discuss this more in Chapter 7.) She was the welcomer. The key to the door of that community. She unlocked the potential of relational networks available in Philippi.

Sometimes you need a breath of fresh air. The first disciples certainly did. Once, they were holed up together in a little room with the doors locked and the windows barred. The room was heavy with the stench of fear, suffocating even. Then Jesus showed up and gave them a breath of fresh air and said, "'Peace be with you. As the Father has sent me, so I send you.'" When he had said this, he breathed on them and said to them, 'Receive the Holy Spirit'" (John 20:21–22).

We are a sent people with the molecules of the risen Jesus infused in our lungs. Breathing with the very breath of heaven, we are called to go into communities—a breath of fresh air. Fresh expressions allow churches who've been holed up in the walls of our inherited churches for too long to go out and be the church in our community. The two can work together in a life-giving exchange.

Picnic Talk

Scripture Focus: Read Acts 16:6–15

1. What impressions do you have after reading Acts 16:6–5? Imagine you are part of this gathering of women down by the river, gathered for prayer. What do you hear, see, notice?

2. What does church look like as described here in Acts 16? What is missing from what you have experienced as church?

3. What are first, second, and third places? Do you think church can happen in those spaces? Why or why not?

4. Do you find the metaphor of a community as an ecosystem helpful? Do you see the potential of planting green spaces as small incarnational micro-communities and how that could possibly impact the larger community?

5. Why do you think fresh expressions of church are more effective at reaching those who have no connection with the existing church?

6. What advantages or disadvantages do you see in the fresh expression form for reaching emerging generations? Why?

7. If all your church does is continue to offer what you currently do, who will not be reached in your community?

CHAPTER 4

The Blended Ecology— Deep Roots

Let's get back to the tree of life! At the center of the blended ecology ecosystem is the tree. Hopefully, you have caught a vision for the tree.

Let us remember the three-ness of this image. This ecosystem is about cultivating the existing tree (Luke 13:6–9) *and* planting the seeds of the trees to come (Matt. 13:1–9) *and* grafting them together in one greater vine-like organism (John 15:1–6).

The tree, the *inherited* church, with its rootedness and depth, resilience and strength, cannot be overcome by the parched context. The wild new life-forms as the *emerging* forms of church in the green spaces, the fresh expressions, tethered to and dependent upon the inherited structure, are cascading into life all throughout the greater ecosystem. A life-giving exchange is happening between the inherited and emerging modes as they are grafted together, creating fresh air for the tree dwellers and new life in the green spaces where there was none before.

A Typical Day in the Blended Ecology

On Sunday morning following our 11:00 a.m. traditional service, I ditch my robe and stole and head out to my next worship experience in jeans and a T-shirt. This gathering meets not in the sanctuary, but in Fat Kats Artistry tattoo parlor in downtown Ocala.

One micro-community we have plugged into at Wildwood is the tattoo culture. Getting tattoos is a huge practice in our society. Nearly four in ten millennials (38 percent) have at least one tattoo, half of those have more than one. Gen Xers are not far behind, with 32 percent claiming to be inked up.[1] As the church, we can ignore this cultural reality or experience transfiguration within it.

There are entire communities built up around this form of artistic expression. What are the chances that someone deeply embedded in the tattoo culture will show up on our doorstep some Sunday morning? Well, highly unlikely, as weekends are the primary time when the tattoo parlor is flourishing. Artists do most of their work on Saturdays and Sundays when potential clients are free from work. Tattoo Parlor Church takes place where that community works and plays.

We worship there, discuss Scripture, serve people on the square experiencing homelessness, and partake of the Lord's Supper, all while we go back and get fresh faith-based symbols inked on our bodies. We inhabit that third place, not to try and get people to come back to a building, but to be the church amid that community. What we find is people are curious. They have questions; they are intrigued. We incarnate the church right in their living room. Not as some imperial powerhouse coming to kick butt and take names, but as a gentle mysterious presence, longing for connection and relationship.

In that tattoo parlor, we have seen people accept Jesus, take Communion for the first time, ask for prayer requests, become disciples, and occasionally ask about what happens back at the inherited mothership where we gather on Sundays. This is happening in movie theaters, pool halls, pubs, community centers, karate dojos, dog parks, yoga studios, and the list goes on ad infinitum all over the United States.

A Blended Ecology Person

Sandra Torchia is with me in the sanctuary. The one with the pews, hymnals, candles, and organs. She is also with me in the tattoo parlor. She is a person of both the tree and the green space. Sandra is one of our pioneers on our go teams, leaders who go into the first, second, and third places to be the church with the people there.

I will never forget the day I watched God heal a man on a park bench through Sandra Torchia. At Tattoo Parlor Church, we were just beginning to do some loving and serving. After being church in the parlor for most of the day, attendees went back into the bay to get fresh cross and flames tattooed on their forearms, hands, and feet. Next, we ventured out onto the downtown Ocala square to prayer walk the area. Many people experiencing homelessness live there and sleep on the park benches and under the gazebos.

We encountered a man there on a park bench with a festering foot wound. You could smell the infection from some distance. He was in a bad way. I consider myself a fairly bold disciple, but I don't hold a candle to Sandra. In this particular gathering, not only did one of our artists accept Christ and receive Communion, but guess who got some ink? Yes, the matriarch herself, Sandra, and another sixty-year-old, precious saint of a woman, D. J. Wenzel, got their first tattoos . . . cross and flames to be exact!

Not only did they get tatted up with Christian symbols, but Sandra, a seventy-four-year-old retired nurse, took radical incarnation to a whole new level. As we were praying with folks and explaining and offering Communion, we encountered this gentleman with the horrible foot wound. After spending some time talking with this man, he asked us to pray for the healing of his foot, indicating he was unable to be on the hospital property for numerous reasons.

Distancing myself from the man's open infection, I timidly laid my hand on his shoulder to pray. Sandra, on the other hand, the retired nurse with her first fresh cross and flame proudly inked on her forearm, got down on her hands and knees to inspect the infected foot up close and personal. She rattled off some orders to some of our younger team members.

In minutes they were back from the drugstore with all the necessary items. On a park bench, outside a tattoo parlor, you could smell the kingdom, as Sandra, on her hands and knees, treated and bandaged this man's infected foot, and potentially saved his life that day. I was watching the Holy Spirit work on this gentleman, as a woman whose name he didn't even know became Jesus to him. As the tears welled up in his eyes, I could sense more than his foot was being healed, but his soul as well. I never saw that man again. I wish I had some incredible turn-around story. But what I know for sure is that the Holy Spirit was powerfully present in that moment, bringing healing in a very real way to a sore person in a sore community.

Fresh expressions release the everyday, ordinary heroes of the faith like Sandra to be the church in the green spaces in our communal ecosystems. All our fresh expressions at

Wildwood are overseen by so-called lay persons; pioneers who were ordained in the grace-filled waters of their baptisms to be the priesthood of all believers. Yes—ordained—just not by a bishop with a stole.

As you can see, there is a life-giving exchange happening here. The inherited church serves as a kind of sending space, a base of operations for the futurefitting project. The latent missionary force sitting in our pews is released again as the apostles, prophets, evangelists, shepherds, and teachers that they are.

The center of the blended ecosystem is the tree—the deeply rooted inherited church. In some ways, each of the places in the ecosystem touch each other and even overlap like a kingdom vine growing everywhere.

Now if we want to futurefit this community with new green spaces, we will need to go and plant seeds in each one of these spheres. This is where the fresh expressions of church come in. While we care for and cultivate a healthy inherited church which is the center of the ecosystem, we also deploy pioneers/cultivators into those first, second, third places to create the new green spaces. So, you may start a network of gatherings in peoples' homes while someone begins a gathering for coworkers in their place of employment, and gathering regularly in one of the third places (i.e., park, community center, restaurant).

Each little green space creates a breath of fresh air, a resurrection environment, where people can encounter the Jesus-centered micro-community.

Let's now take a brief glance at the Scriptures together to recover this narrative, the most pronounced being that of Jerusalem and Antioch in the book of Acts.

The Deepest Story

As Christians, the world does not supply our deepest story, the Bible does. The blended ecology is firmly embedded in the Scriptures. The deepest structural narrative of the community of faith in the Bible is not Jerusalem *or* Antioch, the gathered *or* the scattered, the inherited *or* the missional, the attractional *or* the contextual, it's the *blended ecology*. The blended ecology is a life-giving remix. It's gathered *and* scattered, it's inherited *and* missional, it's attractional *and* contextual, it's deep roots *and* wild branches. It's the life-blood of a singularly diverse God who is always doing a new thing, making a new creation. Again, resurrection itself is a remix. A mash-up of dust and God-breath. Let's begin in the Old Testament and proceed into the New Testament.

Tabernacle, Synagogue, and Temple

One of the first post-fall images the Old Testament reveals for God's "with-ness" as the communal center of humanity is the *tabernacle model*.

God and the people who reflect God are a missional people. We discover God's promise to Abraham to make his descendants "as numerous as the stars in the sky and as the sand on the seashore" will be fulfilled by this new relational arrangement (Gen. 22:17 NIV). God gifted the covenant to the people to offer protective boundaries for their own well-being, and so that they might reflect the actual character of YHWH to all the nations. As covenant people, "a kingdom of priests and a holy nation" (Exod. 19:6 NIV), their rhythms of being will be a "light" to which all the "nations" of the earth will stream (Isa. 60:3).

The locus of God's presence with these redeemed ones was embodied in the tabernacle. This wild God was a mobile force amid the people, a God on the go, leading, guiding, and sustaining the people throughout their wilderness wandering. The tabernacle is designed in such a way that it can be packed up and moved to the next location whenever necessary. Just as God is not stationary but moving, so was the tent that housed God's presence. The mobile community was responsive to the environment, flexible, able to change course at the will of God. There is an idea that the tabernacle is a form of God's with-ness. God's home address, primary residence, *and* God are simultaneously everywhere else in the entire universe.

Once the people crossed over into the promised land, eventually the tabernacle model was replaced with the *temple model*. There was an almost bipolar discussion of the temple in the Old Testament. On one level the concept was almost absurd: "Are you the one to build me a house to live in?" (2 Sam. 7:5) and, "But who is able to build a temple for him, since the heavens, even the highest heavens, cannot contain him?" (2 Chron. 2:6 NIV). On another level, the authors depicted God giving precise instructions about its construction. God seemed to have quite the flair for fashion and interior design, as priestly garments and both tabernacle and temple décor were incredibly elaborate.

In this new temple-centered model, the legitimating narrative was now institutionalized in a stationary place, where the formative stories were reenacted by the professionalized priesthood. The locus of God's power was now centered on a dwelling of magnificent scope and breathtaking architecture, a wonder of the ancient world. The edifice itself would have inspired anyone who beheld it. This was the attractional model extraordinaire!

This shift to a centralized location as the home of YHWH is foundational to an understanding of the attractional model. Faithful adherents to Judaism had to now make the journey to Jerusalem to reenact ritually the legitimating narratives. However, the Babylonian captivity necessitated the emergence of the synagogues, a term synonymous with both a gathering of *people* and a *place* where they gathered.

The *synagogue model* was a both/and kind of structure. The synagogues borrowed from the concept of the tabernacle as a more localized, contextual, religious center, but did not replace the expectation of pilgrimage to the temple. The annual temple pilgrimages grew more complex as the empire expanded, bringing the subjugation of foreign powers.

The New Testament gives us a window into how both temple and synagogue were functioning fully together in the blended ecology way. The temple was the epicenter of the attractional model, the synagogues emerged contextually as communities formed and grew large enough to support the requirements to plant a synagogue. People typically made the temple pilgrimage one to three times each year, but many worshiped at the synagogue every Sabbath.

There is perhaps a compelling portrait of the blended ecology throughout the Old Testament as set forth here. There is theological validation for both the attractional and the contextual, for both the inherited and the emerging forms. We see clear parallels of the gathered and scattered models of community throughout the Old Testament.

Jesus as Enfleshment of the Blended Ecology

It's noteworthy to mention the blended ecology of Jesus' own life and ministry—synagogue and temple, coexisting together. Jesus worked in the fields, and he visited the temple. He preached sermons on the mountains, and he preached in the synagogues. He is the embodiment of both attractional and emerging: the most attractive human being that ever was *and* he was completely dedicated to entering the lives of people where they were.

The incarnation itself is the enfleshment of this, as Jesus descended, to come and move into the neighborhood of our space, to enter our sin-broken lives and shape us through loving relationship (John 1; Phil. 2).

Furthermore, Jesus is the fulfilled embodiment of temple, tabernacle, and Torah. His flesh and blood became the new temple/tabernacle that all the Old Testament pointed toward (Luke 22:19; John 2:19). Jesus synthesized all the models before him into one mega model: a stationary, mobile, enfleshed, incarnational, attractional, emerging flesh-and-blood tabernacle, temple, synagogue—fully human, fully God!

Jesus is a blended ecology, the life of heaven *and* mud-stuff.

Now that Jesus sits on the throne of the cosmos, in all his enfleshed, beautiful, Palestinian, death-conquering self, *and* through the sending of the Holy Spirit, he is "with [us] always" (Matt. 28:20). The church has become the embodiment of everything that Jesus was and is. We are now "the body of Christ" (1 Cor. 12:27) and "temple of the Holy Spirit" (1 Cor. 6:19). Mobile and stationary, attractional and emerging.

The church is a blended ecology, a colony of heaven, in, with, for, and among a sin-marred valley.

Jerusalem and Antioch

So, let's look at where the blended ecology pattern emerged very early in the life of the church—Jerusalem and Antioch.

Jesus, just prior to the ascension, laid out the missional plan: "But you will receive power when the Holy Spirit has come upon you; and you will be my witnesses in Jerusalem, in all Judea and Samaria, and to the ends of the earth" (Acts 1:8). We see that very pattern of the church's growth occur throughout the book of Acts. Pentecost was a remix that enabled Jesus' instructions to develop. There is a clear parallel between the Tower of Babel, with God confusing the languages of humanity, and Pentecost, with God enabling the gospel to be proclaimed in all the native languages of the earth.

The old wild-God of the tabernacle showed up as the wild-child of the Trinity, creating a new tabernacle out of a flesh-and-blood people called the church. The Holy Spirit enabled the disciples to go native, so the bystanders witnessed them speaking in all the "*native*" languages of the world (Acts 2:6, italics mine). The Spirit didn't show up just to create a firework show, but to thrust out the newly born church from the womb of Pentecost.

The very genesis of the Christian movement evidenced the blended ecology structure right from the start. There was the work that needed to be done in Jerusalem, Judea, Samaria, and all the ends of the earth. The initial activity was centered in the temple where the disciples gathered daily, but was also moving out to the edge on the road to Ethiopia (Acts 8:26–27). Very early, a beachhead of the church was established in Jerusalem. The Jewish persecution forced the disciples to move out (Acts 8:1), but they continued to gather and have a presence in Jerusalem. Even during the subsequent outbreaks of Roman imperial persecution, the Jerusalem church moved underground, but existed hidden there just beneath the surface.

Very early in the primitive church, right in the genesis, two distinct brands of the faith began to emerge: Hellenist and Jewish (Acts 6). The church restructured itself to deal with those growing distinctions. The structures of the church formed in response to the nascent missional opportunities. The apostles widely structure around the needs that arose within the community. The structure was not fixed and rigid, but fluid and improvisational.

As the movement spread out to the edges just as Jesus prophetically commanded, different contextual expressions of the faith began to manifest. The first Jerusalem council offered us a model for how the blended ecology can work together in a synergistic way. The early church faced its first huge life-threating issue and was forced to restructure according to the missional need. The bigwigs in Jerusalem (the inherited church) heard that a group of missional renegades were experiencing tremendous growth among the Gentile converts (the emerging church). However, this was a very different church with very different people. Word on the street was, they weren't even being circumcised or following the law! This threatened to tear the whole church apart and destroy the entire movement (Acts 15).

They acted quickly, decisively, and in unity. They also made some huge adjustments. The Gentiles were not willing to put that kind of skin in the game . . . quite literally. Yet for Jews, the circumcision was the mark of a faithful Jewish male, going back to Abraham. You can see this is no small matter, but the early church didn't bat an eye. They responded in a flexible way and moved on. The missional need shaped their decisive action. They had a focused vision on the thing that mattered the most—introducing people to Jesus Christ (Acts 15:1–29).

Essentially, Paul's letters were aimed at institutionalizing what happened at the Jerusalem council in a robust theological system that would guide the life of those emerging communities. Paul's ministry in Acts offered several examples of how the blended ecology worked in the early church.

We see the inherited and emerging church working together. Paul described occasions when he went back to Jerusalem to conference with the leaders there. Those encounters were not always without contention (Gal. 2:11–14). Paul also tried to provide metaphors that described this new reality of deep roots and wild branches, grafted together (Rom. 11:24).

There still today exists a very real tension between inherited and emerging forms of church in the blended ecology way. However, we see the Jerusalem and Antioch models, gathered and scattered, tethered together throughout. There was a synergistic exchange happening as the Jerusalem church heard the stories of Gentiles coming to Christ, and the Antioch model got its authorization and centering from the Jerusalem church (Acts 15).

Paul saw one of his functions as an apostle to the Gentiles out on the missional edge to collect an offering for the church back in Jerusalem. The Jerusalem church seemed to have been struggling and was overwhelmed with people experiencing poverty, and Paul was accessing his relational networks for funding to help.

One can see through Paul's exchanges with Peter and other church leaders that the influencing was not a one-way street. Paul sometimes called the inherited leaders out and they, in turn, at times tried to rein Paul in. Jerusalem was influencing Antioch, and vice versa (Gal. 2). The blended ecology is not healthy if both inherited and emerging forms do not have some influence on the other. As both grow and influence each other, the whole church is strengthened.

In a revitalization, you, too, will have to make some major adjustments. There will be issues that some people are willing to die for or at least leave the church for. You must decide what are the key issues, while maintaining a singular focused vision on reaching not-yet-Christians. The blended ecology allows every church to have a Jerusalem and an Antioch.

Blended Ecology and Resurrection

Within the work of ecosystem cultivation, we have primarily three roles: pioneer, supporter, and permission giver.

Pioneers: People who are passionate about mission on the edges.

Supporters: People who are passionate about supporting and releasing pioneers.

Permission Givers: People who use their role to foster release of pioneers and to influence the system to be more willing to experiment.

Notice Paul's language of seeders, waterers, and harvesters from 1 Corinthians 3:6–9 where he did some remixing of metaphors, blending people, harvest fields, and buildings: "you are God's field, God's building" (v. 9). Maybe these verses are the first vision of urban renewal, futurefitting urban centers with green spaces. This is a vision of the church as a new creation, a sign and foretaste of the urban-garden eco-city we see in Revelation.

The collective effort of these pioneers, supporters, and permission givers has cascading effects on the entire community. We will understand this interaction later through the process of trophic cascades, an ecological phenomenon that is catalyzed by the absence or addition of keystone species (usually predators at the top of a food chain), which often trigger dramatic surging changes in an ecosystem.

Through releasing people in the blended ecology way, relationships are expanded beyond the existing congregation. New persons of peace emerge and new relational networks become accessible. Real communities are beginning to form around work, play, hobbies, and passions. Life-giving exchanges of neighborly good are occurring everywhere throughout the larger communal ecosystem; these interactions also transform the inherited congregation.

In the church world we call this cascading transformation *revitalization*; the remixing of individual ingredients produces a new creation.

The blended ecology way releases revitalization in this sense. The new ecosystem is no longer reducible to the simplicity of the isolated modes themselves. A new creation mosaic is born, a reworking of the existing pieces into a new whole. The same material made new.

The Spirit's remixing of the inherited and emerging modes catalyzes a series of synergistic interactions that unleash the force of resurrection. This new creation requires different kinds of leadership, processes, and practices than most inherited congregations are equipped for.

Let's turn fully now into the how of the blended ecology.

Picnic Talk

Scripture Focus: Read Acts 15:1–35

1. What impressions do you have from Acts 15:1–35? What sticks out the most? Can you see the difference between Jerusalem and Antioch, and yet the unity they share?

2. Do you agree that what's happening in the tattoo parlor and the sanctuary are both a form of church? Why or why not?

3. Do you think your church more resembles the temple model or the tabernacle model? Structurally speaking, are you more Jerusalem, Antioch, or both? Why?

4. What are some of the ways you see your church operating in the Jerusalem, stationary, attractional way?

5. What are the ways you see your church operating in the Antioch, scattered, mobile, emerging way?

6. Can you see the value of being both an attractional and missional church? Why or why not?

7. Where do you feel Jesus spent most of his time? Why do you think he did that?

8. Who are the Gentiles in your community? The Antioch ones who Jerusalem cannot reach? The ones who live in the neighborhood, but are not represented in your congregation?

PART TWO

Cultivating the New Ecosystem

How the Blended Ecology?

CHAPTER 5

Awakening

The sprawling 3,468 square miles of Yellowstone National Park (YNP) expand into three states: Wyoming, Montana, and Idaho. On March 1, 1872, it was established by the United States Congress and signed into law by President Ulysses S. Grant as the first national park in the United States. The park contains incredible variations of wildlife species and unique geothermal features. It is a massive ecosystem featuring many interweaving networks of smaller habitats. The area is protected from hunting, livestock grazing, and resource development.[1]

The Yellowstone ecosystem allows us to research complex natural interactions, supposedly undisturbed by human civilization. Across the largely colonized and urbanized United States, YNP offers us an endless supply of breathtaking vistas and natural landscapes.

However, not everything is as it seems in YNP. Humans have interfered and reengineered Yellowstone for most of the nearly 150 years it has been a state park. Some of our interventions have had a less-than-helpful impact on the natural processes and species, creating at some level an artificial ecosystem.

Wolves and Trophic Cascades

Federal control programs eliminated wolves in the early 1900s, lending to the creation of this artificial ecosystem. Without the wolves, herbivores overgrazed the landscape, and other carnivorous predators reigned free, creating negative chain reactions throughout the larger ecosystem. When the wolves were reintroduced in 1995, it created a trophic cascade that impacted numerous habitats, and literally transformed the physical dimensions of the rivers and land.

Trophic Cascades: An ecological phenomenon that occurs when three or more trophic levels interact. For instance, an increased number of predators affects the number and behavior of herbivores, which in turn affects the flourishing of plant life. A "cascade" can be triggered by the addition or removal of keystone species, which often results in dramatic changes in ecosystem structure and nutrient cycling.[2]

Yellowstone has become a popular example of this phenomenon. You can watch an amazing short video called "How Wolves Change Rivers" at the link provided in the notes.[3] The deer had essentially grazed down most of the vegetation. The wolves preyed upon the deer and offered a

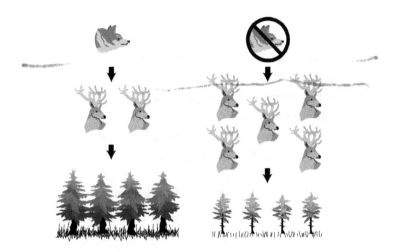

disruption to their feeding patterns. Forests were repopulated. Other species flourished, the artificial ecosystem was revitalized, and the structure of the ecosystem itself was changed. Wolves really do change rivers!

Notice the activity of disruption and initial messiness here. The wolves, as a keystone species at the top of the food chain, created a cascading effect on the deer, other animals, the forests, the vegetation, and eventually the course of the rivers themselves. It is a chain reaction, resulting from the initial disruption that changes the entire network of the ecosystem. While the initial result of wolves preying upon deer caused death and disruption, it also released life and other ecosystem engineers (like beavers) to offer improvisation and innovations that ultimately healed and created a more sustainable ecosystem.

Keystone Species: A species whose behavior impacts multiple other species in an ecosystem. The removal or addition of this species can change the ecosystem drastically.[4]

In the church sphere, all Christians are keystone species in the sense of the five-fold way of apostles, prophets, evangelists, pastors, and teachers (Eph. 4:11).

The Local Church as Artificial Ecosystem

Many local churches have become artificial ecosystems, and fresh expressions provide us a way to release the wolves again.

Declining congregations in the artificial ecosystem scenario are either missing some of the essential keystone species or they have been domesticated into a state of learned helplessness. To experience the remixing power of resurrection, they need to be released.

Jesus perfectly designed the church to thrive in every age and space. While obviously extraneous variables contribute to the decline of an inherited congregation, we need to consider the possibility that some of the decline is of our own making. We have imported a foreign design into the church that is creating this artificial ecosystem.

Initially, it made sense to eliminate wolves from YNP; they are messy predators who kill other species! However, an ecosystem without wolves is an artificial scenario. Again, as seemingly violent and predatory as wolves are, they are necessary life-forms for the health of an ecosystem. Yes, wolves kill deer sometimes, but they also give life in so many other ways. As a keystone species, they shape the behavior of all others in the ecosystem.

The church adopting the attractional-only mode seemed like a good idea and worked well for an extensive period. Full-time, professional pastors paid to care for the massive flocks of already-Christians was great in the Constantinian system. But it is no longer effective and does not reflect the reality of the new missional frontier—a church designed for a jungle must now adapt to the desert.

To try and catalyze revitalization with better organizational leadership and the introduction of new programs is not effective. Resurrection cannot be programed, managed, or owned. There is no one-size-fits-all way to be church or to revitalize one. Rather, a form of revitalization occurs through the four primary moves of cultivating the blended ecology way. *Awakening* the local church to their core identity as the priesthood of all believers and remembering the people in our pews as a missionary force for God—a community of apostles, prophets, evangelists, shepherds, and teachers. *Futurefitting* the congregation to identify these keystone species, teaching them small behaviors of *planting and grafting* that create massive cascading change.

Then *releasing* them to the work of adaptive leadership and ecosystem engineering.

Awakening Your Keystone Species

In order to release a trophic cascade, someone had to decide to bring back the wolves. Someone was awakened to the fact the ecosystem needed wolves, then they acted decisively to reintroduce them.

The first step in cultivating the blended ecology in your community begins not in the green spaces but back at the tree. There are changes that must take place at the inherited church hub for the blended ecology to work. The problem with most revitalization proposals is that they stop there.

Awakening from apostolic amnesia is an appropriate description of this first move. The church has fallen asleep; it's time to awaken. How do we awaken congregations drowning and buried in the sandstorms to see a fresh vision of the tree of life? How do we remember that we are the ones called and sent to plant the gardens that can transform the deserts of decline?

For the blended ecology way to work in the futurefitting of communities and potential revitalization of local churches, there are primarily two places we must focus our attention: the *center* and the *edge*. Jerusalem and Antioch. Let's consider the center as the inherited congregation, and the edge as the fresh expressions of church. I encourage churches to split their time, energy, and resources equally between those two focus areas beginning with the inherited congregation (from Jerusalem, Judea, Samaria, and to the ends of the earth [Acts 1:8]). If the center is not healthy, the whole ecosystem suffers.

Returning to the image of the tree of life, if the tree dies, many of the emerging life-forms will die. They are dependent on the rich nutrients of the deep root system of the tree. Some cannot live without the shade that the tree offers. The current fresh expressions that have demonstrated long-term sustainability are usually tethered to existing congregations. The danger occurs when we become so focused on caring for the tree, we never go out to cast the seeds, or fail to intentionally graft those life-forms together.

Thus, while our starting point is the people in the inherited congregations, the fresh expressions approach provides a powerful vehicle for the (re)missioning of inherited congregations. Just a handful of keystone species can change an entire ecosystem. Jesus heavily invested in a small group of women and men who released a trophic cascade that changed the world. There are times when you may have to go outside the congregation to find a team of people willing to do this work, but as little as two or three people can be your initial team.

What Is Our Why?

Sometimes a local church can forget our why. Simon Sinek speaks of the value of organizations knowing their why: *what we believe that makes us who we are and drives what we do.* It's quite literally why we exist. He goes on to say, "The *why* comes from looking back."[5]

First, an inherited congregation must recover the missional purpose for why we exist.

The conservationists who decided to remove the wolves from YNP probably had good reasons and right intentions, but perhaps they lost sight of why the area of the park became protected in the first place—to conserve a large area of land where wildlife could exist largely unaltered by human civilization.

The church had good reasons for adopting the late-twentieth-century corporate structure. It enabled us to flourish for an extended season in an unprecedented way. Yet, over time, the Christendom way bred an attractional mode of church that is not sustainable in a post-Christian context. When the pews are packed with people every Sunday, building fancy buildings and hiring clergy to take care of them is a no-brainer. The focus was primarily inward—take care of your sheep. Create worship that is worth experiencing so that existing members will invite others from their relational circles.

Yet through adopting this approach we essentially exiled an entire keystone species of leadership. Primarily the apostles, prophets, and evangelists, the people whose giftings are oriented to those outside communities of already-Christians. In this scenario, the why of our existence becomes putting butts in pews. Unfortunately, in this new desert ecosystem no amount of tinkering is going to put butts in pews. This was never the purpose of the church to begin with.

My district superintendent and partner in missional mess-making, Rev. June Edwards, has authorized me to work with the eighty-seven churches in our district to cultivate fresh expressions. In catalyzing revitalization through the blended ecology on a grand scale, she has often reminded our district fresh expressions team that nowhere did Jesus instruct his disciples to build buildings and stick up a sign that says, "Meet us here for an hour on Sundays so we can teach you about the kingdom of God." Jesus sent us out to be the church, a living organism in the world, not to attract people to a church compound.

Remembering for the Future

So how do we go about awakening congregations from our apostolic amnesia? How do we convince our local churches, which may have been existing in the butts-in-pews scenario so long that any other possibility is beyond comprehension? One way to start is with the Remembering for the Future Timeline. This tool, in the Picnic Talk at the conclusion of this chapter, can help your team listen to the congregation and recover your core sent-ness. This exercise creates a habitat of listening, where people can celebrate the joys and voice the frustrations. It will also indicate what you value and point you toward mapping out a future.

Through the process of listening and exchanging questions, you can begin to sense the health of your inherited congregation. You also will begin to see the parts of the past that are obstructing the congregation's future. The decluttering process allows the congregation to have a conversation to strip down to the bare essentials and find their *why*.

To awaken, a congregation needs to recover their central story again. This will require interpretive leadership, a team of people living through a story together, on a journey of sense-making, looking deeper and reestablishing the meaning and purpose of the church.

I want to clarify here what I mean by leadership. Most revitalization strategies fail because they never escape the same institutional thinking that created the problems to begin with, or they advocate that revitalization is all about the skill of a heroic solo leader. This rare breed of turn-around pastor through their deep spirituality, sheer determination, or a bit of workaholism can lead the church out of decline. This sends the signal to most leaders that they aren't good enough, strong enough, or spiritual enough to revitalize a congregation.

I am proposing that churches in need of revitalization don't need more or better inherited mode leadership. That is a large part of the problem that created the decline to begin with. The concept of leadership itself, among many other foundational concepts, must be reconceptualized.

Individuals don't revitalize churches; Spirit-filled communities of Jesus followers do. The kind of leadership I'm referring to is of the utterly relational, "not so with you" lead from below, "servant" variety, not the "exercise authority over" (Matt. 20:20–28 NIV). The Jesus kind. A journey of withness, as the community travels together in the process of becoming, rather than imposing influence from a place of positional leadership as an expert consultant. This leadership emerges from the group, not by self-assertion, but the rational needs of the group to survive and grow.[6]

For instance, rather than envisioning this process as an orchestra, take on the posture of a jazz band. In an orchestra, the conductor stands on a pedestal before the musicians with pre-decided sheet music and a precise plan to be carried out under her leadership. This is an exercise in *causal reasoning*; a predetermined plan is carried out through a series of strategic goals, focused on an expected return.

A jazz leader operates a little differently. Sitting down with the other members, maybe she chooses a tempo and tone, but then they just start to play. They do the creative work together. It is spontaneous, leaving open different possible futures. It is improvisational—who knows where this may end up! It's also more fun. There is still leadership, but each person emerges as a leader in different parts of the song—a non-linear dance of followership and leadership. It's dispersed, polycentric leadership, rather than centered on the direction of an individual. This is an exercise in effectual reasoning, starting with who and what you have and making something new.

Effectual reasoning emphasizes affordable loss; causal reasoning depends upon competitive analyses. Effectual reasoning is built upon strategic partnerships; whereas causal reasoning urges the exploitation of preexisting knowledge and prediction. Effectual reasoning stresses the leveraging of contingencies as they emerge.[7]

In the blended ecology we need both inherited and emerging modes of leadership; it's usually the second that's in short supply or suppressed. In the next chapter I will suggest a design thinking approach for your team. For now, let's use Tod Bolsinger's definition of *leadership* as "energizing a community of people toward their own transformation in order to accomplish a shared mission in the face of a changing world."[8]

Breaking the Toxic Loop

Many churches have fallen into the slumber of becoming internally focused to a toxic degree in an artificial ecosystem. In the attractional model, it is easy to get amnesia over the nature of our sent-ness, the very *why* of our existence. If this amnesia spreads throughout the congregation, one of the essential truths of our Christian faith can become toxic: "'and they will call him Immanuel' (which means 'God with us')" (Matt. 1:23 NIV).

This central core claim can also cast a shadow. Whenever there is an "us," it always creates a "them." Whenever the focus is "I," it can exclude an "other." When all I can see is "me," it creates an invisible "you." When we become so focused on God being with "us," the very inclusive nature of a community that invited sinners, tax collectors, and prostitutes to the table is reversed. We become exclusive, as in God is *only* with "us." You can join us if you look like us, talk like us, and are the same age as us.

When a church has become fixated on this exclusive us-ness, then what I call a *toxic loop* has formed. The toxic loop describes an often unconscious cycle of dysfunction, where a congregation has become entirely "us" fixated to the exclusion of the "them." The only concern in this community is taking care of each other and preserving the status quo of a past that is no longer based in reality. It's like a walled city under siege where the people eat each other rather than shift the orientation outward. Imagine a museum that is owned by a group who would rather die staring at the exhibits than sell tickets to let others inside.

Most churches decline and even die because the "us" of their "God with us" is too small. I believe fresh expressions catalyze revitalizations in existing congregations because they expand the "with-ness" and the "us-ness" of those congregations.

One of the most effective ways to break the loop and awaken a congregation is through planting fresh expressions in the community. A fresh expression forces a congregation to look outside itself. It provides a process to release experimentation on the edge while caring for the center.

This opens the possibility of disruption in an overly stable system, leading us to the *edge of chaos*, which in the innovation framework refers to the sweet spot between enough openness to release change and enough structure to sustain order. Overly stable systems suffocate innovation; conversely too much rapid change destroys systems. Theologically, this is about the liminal space between creation and new creation, opening ourselves to the Spirit bringing forth a new future, while balancing this with the Spirit's activity in the past.[9]

Complexity thinking can help us understand how inherited churches that plant fresh expressions can break the toxic loop and experience revitalization without tearing the whole organization apart.

Complexity thinkers refers to *path dependency*: how the past of an organization directs its future possibilities. Organizations continue to employ a practice or product because of a history of use, even when a new practice or product comes along that is more effective. Simply, it is easier to follow an existing path than to explore the creation of a new one. An *attractor*: refers to a system's direction of travel, or the specific subset of states that a social system may take. This corresponds to the normal behavior toward which it will naturally gravitate. Social systems are organized around these attractors: ideas and practices that have gained support. However, a *strange attractor* refers to a nascent dynamic that arises and pulls an organization in a new direction.[10]

So, the transformation of a system occurs when a strange attractor gathers enough support to successfully challenge the existing pattern of an organization. New attractors create destabilization in the system, and a kind of tug-of-war can occur between old and new. While operating within a certain region of possibility, again determined by path dependency, a multitude of paths become possible within that defined region.[11]

Disruption and mess are not only okay, but necessary to catalyze transformation. The small activities of the fresh expressions begin to draw the whole system in a new direction within those boundaries of possibility. The blended ecology allows every local church to simultaneously harness the power of missional innovation (disruptive solution), while cultivating less drastic change in aging congregations (incremental solution).

More simply, the fresh expressions breaks us open and reconfigures our soul in such a way that it touches our community again. The shift causes us to see and ask who is our other? An "us only" church is corrupted at a fundamental and genetic level.

As Tod Bolsinger says, "Well, how do we change *any* DNA? Through sex."[12] Giving birth to new things. It is not easier to give birth than to raise the dead, but giving birth is often a step in the process of raising the dead. In the blended ecology way, every Christian becomes an ordinary hero in the priesthood of all believers, and every church becomes a multi-site. This is the focus of our remaining chapters.

Picnic Talk

(This Picnic Talk is a single exercise that should happen indoors, with as many members of the existing congregation as possible.)

Remembering for the Future Timeline

Environment: Try to establish a sense of excitement for this gathering. Get as many people present as possible from the existing congregation. Perhaps an after-service potluck,

Wednesday night fellowship dinner, etc. Make great strides to have the different constituencies of your congregation present.

Materials: You will need a roll of stick-up paper (or you can post a series of large stick-up notes slightly overlapping), multiple colored markers, and a clear wall space with no obstructions.

Instructions: Draw a single line across the entirety of the wall in advance of the gathering. Identify three major points on the timeline:

- The Beginning (Write "The Beginning" in the first part of the timeline; leave enough room for people to fill in memories around this point.)
- Now (Go about three-quarters down the line and write, "Now," with space for people to write in memories.)
- The Future (Leave the final quarter of the timeline for visioning; write "The Future.")

Exercise: Have people come up and share significant memories they have in the life of the church: weddings, funerals, homecomings, outreaches, crusades, revivals, whatever! If the beginning of the congregation is beyond the living memory of the church, ask folks to fill in what details they know. Try to flesh out who, what, where, when, and how.

Once the timeline is well-populated up until "Now," next have folks come forward and share what dreams they have for the future of the church.

Celebrate each contribution; don't make any judgments. Just share in the joy of remembering and visioning.

The Remembering for the Future Timeline is a listening tool, to understand the congregation and their memories, hopes, and dreams. It gives them a chance to be heard, and gives the leadership an opportunity to listen, learn, and love. If all significant moments are "inward" focused (i.e., pastor _____ came, _____ got married, we renovated the fellowship hall, etc.) and there are no #_____ got baptized, started new outreach, had a community revival, neighborhood campaign, mission trip, etc., this could be revealing regarding the congregation's inward or outward focus. This information will also be helpful, as you call people back to their apostolic beginnings, significant moments, and dreams for the future. Record this information and keep the timeline for later use.

CHAPTER 6

Futurefitting

God is using the church as an instrument to futurefit the world now with the life of heaven. The Spirit is forming communities that are beginning to reflect the urban-garden, tree-of-life scenario to come.

Futurefitting is about restructuring the local church to reflect the diverse singularity of the triune God and the deeper story of temple and tabernacle, Jerusalem and Antioch, deep roots and wild branches. Or more simply, restructuring local churches for mission.

Structures matter. Jesus warns us about pouring new wine into old wineskins. In the process of fermentation and expansion, the new wine would burst the skins. We put new wine into new wineskins, so the fresh, flexible skin can hold and deliver the expanding wine. So "new wine is put into fresh wineskins, and so both are preserved" (Matt. 9:17). Notice the focus is to preserve *both/and* the new and old wine. We need that fine vintage (attractional) stuff, and the fresh (emerging) stuff. The content stays the same, the container/structure/form changes.

The blended ecology allows local churches to dispense both the fresh and vintage forms of wine. Existing congregations restructured in the blended ecology way can join the disruptive work of the Spirit and release innovation through the employment of dispersed leadership and experimentation. In discussing a missional ministry for a missional church, Alan Hirsh reveals the breakdown often occurs at a structural level because people are unwilling "to reconfigure ministry to suit the missional context."[1]

Unlike the Masdar City project, most of us do not have the luxury of starting over and designing the eco-city from scratch. Our work is more reflective of those engineers tasked with retrofitting cities with new green technologies. Once we become aware of the pollution and lack of sustainability, we are faced with an adaptive challenge. We cannot scrap the city and start over; we must work with what we have and introduce incremental changes that will transform the urban ecosystem.

Again, in the realm of taking declining inherited congregations and refitting the communal ecosystem for resurrection, futurefitting is a more appropriate description. The Spirit is rewiring the community with God's future life now.

If we accept the premise that resurrection is a remix, the power of God to take what was and reconfigure it in a splendid new creation, then for churches to experience revitalization we are going to need a remix of our current structure.

Let's again call to mind both temple *and* tabernacle, Jerusalem *and* Antioch, as we dig into the practicality of futurefitting.

Our primary challenge is not to do Jerusalem better. In fact, there are much better resources regarding how to do the attractional model of church better. The real question that we must now turn to is: How do we do Antioch? How do we cultivate and release the kind of emerging forms of church we see in the book of Acts? How do we tend the relationship between the inherited and emerging forms?

Here are some suggestions to futurefit your church for the blended ecology.

1. Reimagining Revitalization

Futurefitting begins with leadership in the inherited church. Antioch started in Jerusalem. The death of Stephen and the oncoming persecution of the gathered church gives birth to the scattered church (Acts 11:19). This is exactly the way Jesus envisioned and structured the movement to take place (Acts 1:8). While Antioch becomes the church in all its fullness, it also stays connected with and gains authority from Jerusalem. The two support each other in a symbiotic way (Acts 11:22, 26–27; 15).

However, futurefitting is more than an attempt to revitalize dying churches. The purpose is bigger than that. It's more about cultivating transformation in the larger communal ecosystem.

Makoto Fujimura is an artist and author who works in the International Arts Movement. In *Culture Care: Reconnecting with Beauty for Our Common Life,* Fujimura challenges us to reimage culture not as a territory to win, but a garden ecosystem to tend and steward. He challenges the zeitgeist of consumeristic pursuit and warns of the danger of losing our identity as creators who are reflections of the creator God.

What if local churches did not see their communities as something to fix, win, and convert, but rather a cultural ecosystem to steward and cultivate? What if we were to understand mission more as a collaborative art than a science, and the unique role of the artist as what Fujimura describes as *mearcstapas* the "border-stalkers."[2] To reenvision revitalization as cultivating new ecosystems, we need to break free from the corporate emphasis of initiating programs. The *mearcstapas* (an Old English term from *Beowulf*) aptly describes the kind of adaptive leadership your team needs. These border-stalkers of the ancient tribes lived on the edges of their groups, moved in and out, and brought back news. Like the *mearcstapa*s, you will need to inhabit the liminal space, and incarnate the role of helping fragmented cultural tribes find hope and reconciliation.[3]

As border-stalkers you live in the gap between Jerusalem and Antioch, holding those ways together in creative tension. We are just enough part of the congregation that we can provide care, guidance, and leadership while also providing the same in the larger communal ecosystem.

Border-stalkers must live in multiple habitats at once. They can move freely between the relational networks. They are mobile and sent, living in a state of motion. Along the journey they build significant relational connections in the various tribes, but their identity is not limited to any single tribe. They must have the capacity to join these hyper-mobile tribes moving through the space of flows created by technology and be an incarnational presence there, as well as being with the stationary folks who have made a home in the inherited system. In Fresh Expressions US, we call border-stalkers "pioneers."

Jesus was the ultimate *mearcstapa*. He danced between the borders of heaven and earth in the incarnation. He moved among the people, both at the synagogues and on the hillsides. He not only extended love to the children of Israel, but to Samaritans, Roman centurions, Syrophoenician women, sinners, tax-collectors, priests, and prostitutes. He moved in and out of the tribes, bringing hope and reconciliation. He was the enfleshment of both temple and tabernacle.

As a presence in Jerusalem, *you* are invaluable to this resurrection remix process. You are a keystone species within our mega metaphor of ecosystem cultivation. Your behaviors and words have significant impact on the entire ecosystem. If you are a traditional congregation on the new missional frontier, you are going to have to do some evolving for all this to work.

2. Rewiring the Local Church 50/50: Jerusalem and Antioch

Restructuring allows churches to carve out time for local experimentation. Many times, all our time becomes consumed sustaining all the programs of the inherited system. This makes planting fresh expressions of church throughout the community challenging. A good and simple rule of thumb is the 50/50 rule. Fifty percent of our time needs to be structured toward taking care of the congregation. Fifty percent of our time needs to be spent as missionaries in the community. That means for whatever number of hours our church is active, we need to divide our time in this way.

The whole church must restructure itself to focus half our energy on caring for the tree and half our energy planting fresh expressions in the community.

A growing problem for many leaders is the inability of churches to support full-time clergy. Full-time pastors are becoming a luxury to most congregations. In the future, there will be an increasing number of bi-vocational clergy—tent-makers like Paul the apostle. However, we all know there's no such thing as a part-time pastor. Congregations have expectations of their ministers, some that stream back for many decades to the golden age of Christendom. There is an expectation that the pastor is always on call.

Revitalization is not birthed by placing more expectations on already-exhausted clergy.

We need to set clergy free from those Christendom expectations for revitalization to occur: 50 percent of their time spent cultivating the inherited congregation with the other 50 percent being out in the community at large. This is time to simply be in third places, to pray, observe, and encounter.

Consistent presence in those spaces can open all kinds of opportunities. This is not just a rule of thumb for the appointed leader. The leader is modeling the behavior we want to see manifest in all staff and the congregation at large. Everyone in the church must divide their time in the 50/50 way. The leaders of the congregation are establishing behavioral patterns in the congregation through modeling.

Don't have all your meetings at the church compound! Meet in a restaurant, park, or coffee shop. If you encounter people in those spaces, engage them. Always ask staff of establishments if they need anything. Ask your servers if there is anything you can pray for them as you bless the food (and make sure you tip well if you do!).

Do you have Wednesday night Bible study meeting at the church facility? Why not move out into a public venue? Need to visit with potential new members? Go to their homes. Cancel church functions on the grounds to encourage the congregation to attend community gatherings. Meet with people at their jobs when possible. Do staff meetings have to take place in the office? Do you already have a connection with a local business owner who would welcome you to gather in their space? Everything you can do out in the community or in someone's home, do it!

Churches that live into this blended ecology way are also seeing the emergence of a new kind of co-vocational leader. Bi-vocational, with the prefix "bi-" as *twice*, *double*, or *dual*, literally "two voices" or callings, describes persons who serve a local church and maintain employment at another job. Co-vocational, with the prefix "co-" as *with*, or *together*, literally as "with voice" or a "with-ness" calling, describes persons who turn their work place into church. For example, my friend Shawn Mickschl, a self-described "seminary fail-out" who works as a server in a local Kentucky restaurant, pastors a fresh expression of church for fellow servers and patrons of that space. His focus is not to get them to attend a church service, but to be church with them there. Cultivating fresh expressions can transform the inherited congregation into a training hub for co-vocational persons, releasing every Christian to become a minister.

3. Restructuring the Inherited Leadership System: Gather, Grow, Go

To implement the 50/50 concept throughout the congregation, the leadership of the local church will typically need to be restructured. Most congregations are hardwired for Christendom. They operate primarily in the attractional mode. Committees, teams, and processes were structured under the Christendom assumptions, so the majority of the energy and time is dedicated to the internal protocols and processes. If a church does have a missions committee, it is probably focused on mission work *over there*. It may be concerned with the support of missionaries in other countries or organizing the annual out-of-country mission trip, for example.

On the new missional frontier, leadership must be reoriented around local mission. The local church is on the mission field. When you walk out to the parking lot, you are in the third largest mission field in the world. In denominational contexts, you may need to get permission to reorganize the leadership structures of the local church from whatever hierarchal authority that oversees your church. Many local congregations I've worked with have maintained the old committees and, therefore, met denominational requirements, but have created new leadership teams beside those existing committees.

At Wildwood, we stripped down our why to what we call the three Gs: gather, grow, go. We believe it captures the four essential marks, or ingredients, of the church throughout all time and the prominent themes permeating Scripture. So, we *gather* as a community of believers (a community that is *one* and *catholic*), we *grow* in love for God and neighbor (a *holy* community), and we then *go* (a community *sent* in mission). We see from cover to cover in the Bible the themes of community, holiness, and mission.

With our new and simplified vision, we soon realized that our inherited leadership structures did not lend themselves to our purpose. Most meetings were about reading minutes of previous meetings and making internal decisions about the inner life of the church. Mission was something we paid others to do.

Now our leadership structures flow from our threefold purpose. We have a gather team, concerned with forming community in many ways; a grow team, concerned with discipling people in Christ; and a go team, focused solely on engaging the mission field around us. Each area is just as vital and important. Being structured in this way allows us to create space for experimentation in the community.

4. Forming the Team: Quality Care and Disruptive Innovation Departments

A practical way to think about cultivating the blended ecology in local congregations is to embrace this concept of Jerusalem *and* Antioch. To borrow from the language of the business world, you can think of your church as having primarily two departments. One department is all about Jerusalem, caring for the inherited congregation. You can think of this as your quality care department. Any organization that doesn't take care of its existing customers won't be around long. At the same time, taking the lead of some of the larger proactive corporations, you need to a create a disruptive innovation department.

There is no quick fix. Local churches cannot be reoriented around mission overnight. That is not a realistic expectation in most inherited congregations. It is much easier in a church plant when you build that into the DNA from the beginning. In the inherited congregation, an apostolic awakening must take place first. In my experience, mission is like a virus that spreads throughout the body, but it must start somewhere. Creating a team specifically for that function is essential. Dream big, start small.

While most of the committees, teams, and meetings will be focused on quality care, identifying some of your key leaders to start a new department is a simple change that can have massive impact. This is your Antioch team. These are the border-stalkers you want to collaborate with and invite to explore innovation and experimentation. This gives every church an opportunity to create a research-and-development division within the inherited system and break the toxic loop.

You need to identify your keystone species for this team. Some of them are already in your church, but not all of them.

Many churches have non-functioning or barely functioning evangelism committees. These committees can easily be futurefitted to become the fresh expressions team. Make it clear from the outset that this department will be involved in risk-taking experimentation. They will need people who are willing to engage in the disruptive work of mess-making.

On the new missional frontier, there is no room for heroic solo leaders. Lone wolves become just wolves. You are going to need a team.

The team needs people who fill each of the essential roles: pioneers, supporters, and permission givers. You also need to begin identifying potential persons of peace. You may find it helpful to structure the team in the following way.

You want your solid and devoted Christians, those who are mature in their faith, as the core of the team, if you will. Most of the time, those folks have little connection to

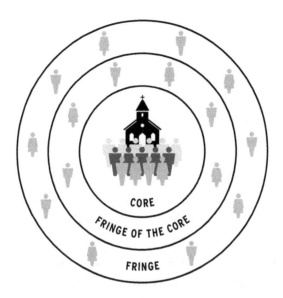

people beyond the local church. We have done such a great job creating an alternative community in the world, we have lost connection with the community around us.

But you also want to have some people on this team who are newer Christians and maybe not even members of your church. Maybe they are just exploring. Inviting these people on the fringe of the core is vital. They often still have connections with relational networks in the community and may even have access to the persons of peace. They also bring a unique perspective. Like the border-stalker, they have a vantage point that others in the core may not have.

Finally, you to want to have people on the team who may or may not even be Christian. These are people on the fringe. These folks most likely have no connection to your church at all. They may even become the persons of peace themselves. The perspective they bring is crucial to the whole venture. They can keep the team from speaking Christianese or falling into the trap of fixing, taking, and winning our community back. They may be the ones who open access to the third places in the community.

5. The "Work" of the Team—Design Thinking

The number-one problem of most churches: they never start. Every time I'm coaching a church through the process of adapting for the blended ecology way, it happens. The moment when someone in the group falls into the institutional mode of thinking. They ask questions like, How will we measure? How much will it cost? What will we do when happens? Will those people in the fresh expressions ever come back here to *real* church? These well-meaning questions can paralyze any forward progress.

In the West, we are programmed to figure out all the answers before we start (causal reasoning). On a journey, we like to know every turn, how many stop signs, U-turns, and traffic delays we will have. Fresh expressions don't work this way. The early church didn't have all the answers; they just started and trusted the Holy Spirit (effectual reasoning).

I want to suggest that design thinking provides a strong framework for your team to utilize.

Design Thinking is a model of thought and reflection centered on people. It refers to design-specific cognitive activities applied *during* the process of designing. This methodology is widely used as a tool across disciplines. One prominent motto in this framework: "fail early in order to succeed sooner."[4]

Failing forward faster is a foundational design thinking principle that helps to maximize learning and insights crucial for human-centered innovation. The focus on collaborative work in small groups where everyone is fueling the creative capacity of the team is part of the magic of the design thinking process.

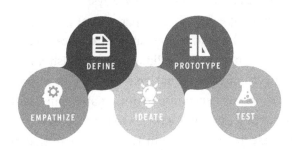

(A) Empathize: The team must first gain an empathic understanding of the people we are trying to reach. Who is our other and how can we be with them? What struggles do they face, and how can we be a withness within those realities? In the fresh expressions journey, this is about listening, then loving and serving.

(B) Define: This is a journey of understanding what's sore in the community. What are the needs here? How do we come together in a mutual exchange of blessing to find healing together? How do we offer communal life with Jesus, and love and serve each other around the sore spots?

(C) Ideate: This is about asking "what if" with our eyes toward God's promised hope for the future. There are many techniques to cultivate healthy brainstorming sessions, but the main idea is for the team to come up with as many ideas as possible, and nothing is too outside the box. Prayerfully, we now ask how God is calling us to form community with new people, in new places, and new ways.

(D) Prototype: This is an experimental phase, in which we get out in the first, second, and third places and simply try stuff. We use prayer walking and establish a small go team to become an incarnational presence in a space. We pray, observe, and encounter. Form relationships with the persons of peace who grant access to those spaces.

(E) Test: It's important to remember here that this is a non-linear process, so we remain reflexive as we move through the interweaving stages. It is a fluid process, in which the team will flow and recycle in different directions. The test stage involves iterating frequently based on continuous feedback, experimenting, failing, and using improvisation as you go. Start trying stuff!

This methodology helps to eradicate the complexity and disorder in the initial stages that usually paralyze churches from starting to engage their community. The advantage of design thinking allows the team to immerse themselves in a problem to innovate a potential solution. We start from the perspective of the people we are seeking to be with. It is in essence an incarnational approach. The emerging forms of church take shape in a collaborative process, where responsibilities are shared among the team and the host culture.

The process involves iterating frequently based on continuous feedback, experimenting, failing, and using improvisation as you go. It is often not a neat, clean process in the sense of thinking through all the potential implications then starting. It is starting, then dealing with emergent implications as they arise.

This process also untangles us from outdated missional methodologies in which we view the larger community and its people as a problem we can fix and shifts us into joining the people in their reality, working together in an adaptive way to bring healing to the community. It's messy stuff; one that requires a particularly artistic approach to creativity.

The small changes emerging from the experimentation of your fresh expressions team will be amplified through the grafting (feedback loops) we will discuss later. Don't underestimate the power of these seemingly small developments. They will become the strange attractor that draws the whole system in a new direction over time.

Maybe Nike was onto something as a good motto for your team: "Just do it!"

Picnic Talk

Design Thinking Exercise

The Marshmallow Tower Challenge

Purpose: This challenge encourages the design thinking mind-set and creates team synergy.

With the simple ingredients and eighteen minutes, your team must build the tallest possible tower that can support the weight of a marshmallow. Primarily the exercise forces the team to build through repeated iterations . . . failing forward faster.

Instructions:

1. Gather all the interested parties who could become your fresh expressions team.

2. Provide the following materials for each team:
   - 20 sticks of dry spaghetti
   - One yard of string
   - One yard of tape

- One marshmallow
- Measuring tape

3. Divide teams into groups of four. Explain the challenge: build the tallest tower possible in eighteen minutes that will support the marshmallow.

4. Set a timer . . . then just do it!

5. Measure each team's structure.

6. Ask each team to describe their process.

7. Show the team this TED Talk from Tom Wujec when they have concluded the exercise: https://www.ted.com/talks/tom_wujec_build_a_tower?language=en#t-392563.

8. Process the talk together. Did you find this exercise helpful in shifting into an experimental, people-centered, fresh expressions approach?

CHAPTER 7
Cultivating and Grafting

Now that we have organized a team and futurefitted the inherited congregation for mission, it's time to move into planting fresh expressions—futurefitting the community with the life of heaven. How do we go out and join Jesus in the cultivation of incarnational communities in the flows of a networked, mobile, post-everything, hyperconnected world?

To open this chapter, stop and read Luke 10:1–12. If there is a single passage that undergirds what the fresh expressions movement seems to be about and gives us a missional blueprint on how to join with the Holy Spirit, this is it. We will extract processes and practices from this passage as we go along.

So, here's an overview of how the process typically works. While there are variations, this is a good outline to follow.

underpinned by prayer, on-going listening, and relationships with the wider church

Stage 1: Listening

The first stage of planting fresh expressions within the community cannot be overemphasized. In the blended ecology, we are listening to God, the inherited congregation, and the larger community.

This needs to be an intentional focus of the team from the beginning. Spending time in prayer together, studying Scripture together, and checking in with each other about what people are hearing God say—this is all essential work of the team. Unfortunately, many people pass right over this step and pay for it in the long haul, partly because we are not very good at listening in the West. We are hardwired by our culture not to listen.

When we created the North Central District Fresh Expressions Team, a group responsible for helping culti-vate fresh expressions among eighty-seven local churches, we started our work with a collaborative "Luke 10:02 Prayer Initiative." Not only did we commit to intentionally pray each day the missional prayer of Jesus, "The harvest is plentiful, but the workers are few. Ask the Lord of the harvest, therefore, to send out workers into his harvest field" (NIV), we invited the whole district—which at that time consisted of an average Sunday worship attendance of about 13,628 United Methodists—to join us in prayer at 10:02 a.m. or some set time throughout their day. There are now more than seventy fresh expressions in our district alone, the greatest concentration of fresh expressions in the United States. Our entire district is now a massive blended ecology ecosystem. Building our efforts on the foundation of prayer cannot be overstated.

This is a simple tool that churches can use to undergird their work with prayer. Simply pause together each day to pray specifically the missional prayer of Jesus.

Who Is Our Other?

There is great value in using every demographic tool available to listen to the congregation and community: Natural Church Development, MissionInsite, Peoplegroups.info, and many others. We need to understand the mission field around our church and the people there, but those instruments must be combined with some simple boots-on-the-ground tools.

I believe every fresh expression should start with a single question: Who is our *other?* Who do we see in the community around us that we don't see in our church? Every time there is an "us," it always creates a "them." Every time there is a clearly defined "we," it always creates an excluded "they." Every time our "I" is too big, it always creates an "other." This other-orientation is the default mode of fresh expressions. We cannot have true rapport without the kenotic self-emptying that Christ embodies in the incarnation (Phil. 2:1–11), what Jesus calls "deny[ing]" self (Matt. 16:24).

Who is our *other* and how can we be *with* them? Fresh expressions don't begin with a desire to win, manage, own, or fix the people in our community, but to enter their world in incarnational, natural ways to cultivate relationships.

What Is Sore *in Our Neighborhoods and Networks?*

My friend Verlon Fosner uses the terminology of "sore neighborhoods" in his pioneering work with The Dinner Church Collective. He advocates that local churches need to return to a neighborhood theology: a theology of place (also known as the parish model). He points out how most churches have embraced the church-growth movement principles, with little regard to the actual makeup of the neighborhoods where they live. This has contributed to the decline of the US church. By returning to theology of the neighborhood, churches exist to know and serve the greatest needs of their immediate neighbors.[1]

In a network society connected by flows, we can see our community as a series of interconnected neighborhoods or even micro-communities. We can expand the understanding of neighborhood to include places and practices in a larger network, rather than confining it to geography alone. These are communal habitats within the larger missional ecosystem. In the blended ecology, we need both a theology of the neighborhood and a theology of the network. The inherited mode primarily serves the larger mission of the neighborhood; the emerging mode the larger mission of the network. What does soreness look like in this remixed scenario?

Sore communities are those where there exists significant populations of the marginalized and lonely. One reason why dinner churches are springing up everywhere is because they have simply plugged into two primary felt needs: hunger and isolation. I discussed the emerging economic reality and the hollowing of the middle earlier. Why are churches still targeting a middle class that largely no longer exists when so many American families visit food banks and live below the poverty line?

Although prevalent, poverty is not always the only kind of soreness. I firmly believe every community is sore in some way. Even in affluent communities, there is some ache that God desires to heal. In The Villages, Florida, the retirement community where I served as the associate pastor of New Covenant United Methodist Church for four years, there is a different kind of sore. There are people there who secretly show up to our food pantry, but the major demographic of this retirement community is affluent.

By all outward appearances, The Villages is eerily like *The Truman Show*. Everything is manicured to perfection and people cruise around in golf carts, enjoying the fruits of their retirement. There is a seeming artificiality to it all. However, my major focus at New Covenant was to plant a Celebrate Recovery program. Thus, I worked amidst the dark underbelly of The Villages, "Florida's Friendliest Hometown." Some think this pristine gated community would be absent of typical sinfulness elsewhere. This is a false assumption—prostitution, alcoholism, and addiction exist just below the well-polished surface. Death, abandonment, and loneliness exist in all communities. This is a sore community, but in a different way.

The greatest soreness in a network society is isolation. People are connected in blazing 5G speed all the time, and yet isolated, longing for authentic connection. Isn't that really what sin and the fall are all about? The shattering of relationships that leave one alone. The greatest brokenness of our human condition is the fragmentation of our relationship with God and each other that results from our willful disobedience. Human beings of all races, ages, and socioeconomic status experience the soreness of isolation to some extent.

Within this scenario, the church can offer the world the greatest gift of all, in fact the only gift we can offer that no other organization can—communal life with Jesus. The life that heals our isolation.

As we are in the process of double listening to our communities, we are seeking to find the sore places that we can love and serve. Prayerfully seeking to form communities of Jesus with people where they work and play.

Prayer Walk

Getting out in the spaces to pray will help you identify *others, practices,* and *places* in the community. The old/new practice of prayer walking has incredible potential when done in a posture of listening. This is a simple way to mobilize God's mission force and get people out in the community. The key is to keep it simple. We suggest focusing on three basic practices: pray, observe, encounter.

Pray: This is simply about putting sneakers on your prayers. Walking around having a conversation with God, sensitizing one's self to the stirrings of the Holy Spirit. If you feel God nudging you to pray for a specific home, business, or school—do it! Pray over the streets, pray over the buildings, pray over the people. Sometimes I like to pray, "God, show me what's breaking your heart in this space. What is sore here?" And then quietly listen.

Observation: This is simply a form of listening. How many people do you notice in the space? What are they doing? What are the conditions of the neighborhoods where you are? What kinds of isolation do you see? What kind of practices are people participating in? Are people engaging each other in certain ways? How are they dressed? What ways do you see the Holy Spirit at work? What is God up to here?

Encounter: This one is the scariest for people who may not be strong extroverts with evangelistic giftings. Here's the good news: you don't have to encounter anyone unless they engage with you or unless God tells you to! More good news: encountering is not about, "Hey, Brother, if you died today do you know your eternal destination?" And it's also not about a Romans road, sinner's prayer, or any of that other business. Nor is it about holding up "Jesus saves" signs or blowing on bull horns. When God brings someone into your path and the Spirit nudges toward encounter, start with, "Hello! What's your name? How are you doing today?" If someone inquires about your activity, let them know you are just out praying for the community and ask, "Is there anything I can pray for you?"

That's it. No bells and whistles. No fancy evangelism tactics; just pray, observe, and encounter.

Who Is Our Sacagawea?: Identifying the Person of Peace

As we go out in teams sent by Jesus, we become the answer to our own prayer (Luke 10:2). Jesus doesn't sugarcoat it. He lets us know we are often going into hostile territory, like sheep among wolves. Again, the key is to travel light. We leave the baggage behind. We come empty-handed in a posture of listening to do life with the people we find there. To join our *other* in *with-ness.*

Tod Bolsinger, in his book *Canoeing the Mountains,* retraced the footsteps of the explorers Lewis and Clark as an analogy for the kind of leadership we need in uncharted territory. Initially one may struggle with this analogy, as it seemingly assumes the eurotribal narrative of brave pioneers journeying out to map and master the unknown. The very Western Christendom story of conquering, boldly going where no one has gone before. Only that's not true of Lewis and Clark, and it's not true of us either. People had already braved the Continental Divide and the Rocky Mountains and settled along the Pacific Coast long ago.

Bolsinger came to a profound truth when he began to describe the Native American woman who accompanied Lewis and Clark, Sacagawea. He says, "Sacagawea was not venturing into unexplored territory, she was going home."[2] It wasn't some bold frontier to be conquered for this young nursing mother, it was the native land of her ancestors. In the Lewis and Clark expedition, she was able to connect them to the horses and resources they needed, translate between the tribes, and navigate the tense encounters. This woman led alongside the group, endured everything they endured, and had a voice in the decision-making.

In Jesus' missional blueprint, we would call Sacagawea our *person of peace*. This is the person who calls our "uncharted territory" simply "home." This is the person who Jesus says to find and stay with. Receive their peace and let them receive yours. Notice the reciprocal language of Jesus, if they "[share] in peace, your peace will rest on that person" (Luke 10:6). It's not just us bringing to them something they need; they also have what we need. There is a language of exchange, not superiority or dominance.

These are the people who give us an entryway into the community to which we are sent; they translate, contribute, and lead alongside. They open the door to relational potential of that community and they show us "the way things are done around here." They are the welcomers who offer a safe place. They invite us to the table to be with. They offer us a gift by sharing their lives with us. They teach us the language and the customs of the tribe. As the border-stalkers, we bring good news and presence, but they give us the space to be. It is a reciprocal exchange of blessing and peace.

Lewis and Clark likely wouldn't have survived without the skills, language, and presence of Sacagawea. I know for sure that fresh expressions cannot survive without a person of peace. Without the person of peace, we are simply employing another imperial conquering tactic.

Once we have listened to God and our community, once we have been invited into the relational network, this moves us into the loving and serving stage of a fresh expression. What Luke 10 describes as eating, staying, and healing.

Stage 2: Loving/Serving

In the Luke 10 missional blueprint, there is the instruction: "Whenever you enter a town and its people welcome you . . . cure the sick who are there" (vv. 8–9). Again, I see the language of mutuality. We are dependent upon the welcoming of the people; we also become conduits of the Holy Spirit to cure the sick. Every community is sore and God wants to use the church as an instrument of healing and reconciliation.

This serving develops organically from our sincere desire to listen. This serving is not manipulative or patronizing; it is not oriented toward fixing the other.

It's imperative that we establish this call to cure on the foundation of building meaningful relationships. As we are welcomed in, doing life with, there is a kind of healing that takes place. The healing often takes the form of loving and serving the people we find there. If the greatest soreness of the sin-fragmented soul is isolation, separating ourselves from God and each other, then the first cure that takes place is the healing that comes through loving and serving each other.

This is not a program to revitalize our church; it's a missional posture that enables us to love our neighbor. Once we understand this dynamic, as needs emerge within the community, we can work together to meet those needs.

Stage 3: Building Community

In Luke 10, there is strong relational language of abiding: "Remain in the same house, eating and drinking whatever they provide. . . . Do not move about from house to house" (v. 7). Leonard Sweet reminds us, "The story of Christianity didn't take shape behind pulpits or on altars or in books. No, the story of Christianity takes shape around tables, as people face one another as equals, telling stories, sharing memories, enjoying food with one another."[3] This idea of sharing life, breaking bread, and being the church in the places where life happens is prominent in Jesus' missional blueprint. In fresh expressions we call this activity "building community."

It is through the repeated patterns of with-ness that loving and serving becomes authentic community. Relationships gain strength over time and trust begins to build among the group.

A profound sense of connectedness begins to form as we gather around the habitual practices. The community becomes a source of life as we experience the healing of our isolation. Not only do we enjoy being around each other, but it becomes something we look forward to. The relationships have grown beyond whatever hobby, passion, or activity may have initially connected the group. Our sense of purpose and identity among the micro-community finds its fullest expression as we become more and more free to be. We start to find an authentic sense of *belonging*.

There is no bullet-point list we can check as we move through the process. There is no clearly defined protocol, "When this occurs, do this." We are often operating in the realm of intuition, under the nudging of the Holy Spirit.

Many times, we find that relationships are forming simultaneously with the exploration of faith. Once we sense this kind of belonging and community has formed, we begin to evolve organically into the next stage.

Stage 4: Exploring Discipleship

In this stage, the community begins to grapple with Jesus' statement, "The kingdom of God has come near to you" (v. 9). This is where we begin to wrestle with what it means to live under the lordship of Jesus and become citizens of his kingdom. The group begins to intentionally explore the Christian faith. This occurs through a mixture of both formal learning (intentional conversations) and social learning (simply sharing in the rhythms of life together). More mature believers may begin to form mentorships with younger apprentices, spending time outside the group, discipling them through the messy relational process. There is no formal program, no seven steps to make a disciple. We are operating primarily in the realm of improvisation, sensitive to the nudging of the Holy Spirit, responding and adjusting as we go.

This kind of evangelism requires us to be sensitive to the fact that God is already at work in every life. We are not simply trying to manipulate someone into a decision for Christ as if they were a notch on our belt. We are being present with people, paying attention, and responding to the movement of the Spirit as we go on the journey together. We are experiencing the unfolding of the good news together, in real time.

Graham Cray reminds us that "Evangelism and disciple-making are inseparable. Evangelism calls people to lifelong discipleship by setting before them a way of life, as a follower of Christ the king."[4] This is utterly a relational approach to discipleship. Jesus models this for us throughout the Gospels, befriending and journeying beside people of various walks of life. Through their relationship with Jesus, they are experiencing a profound transformation.

Sometimes this is the most difficult transition to make within a fresh expression. Many of the leaders I consult with are not satisfied with the language of "messy relationship" and "Spirit nudges." We are wired for steps and procedures and we want to be able to measure and replicate. Unfortunately, forming disciples of Jesus simply doesn't work that way. Each context is different, and there are multiple extraneous variables to consider for each person involved.

When disciples of Christ are beginning to be formed, we are moving fully into *ecclesia*, a community centered around the risen Jesus, a.k.a. church.

Stage 5: Church Taking Shape

When people are beginning to enter into relationship with Christ, reorient their lives around the risen Jesus, and become passionate about serving others, church is taking shape. This may not appear to be our conventional understanding of church. Each fresh expression may be as diverse as the group or practice it is centered around, but as the marks of the church begin to emerge, these churches in the flows are missional, formational, contextual, and ecclesial.

Journeying with and among these mobile tribes in the daily networks centered on shared practices forces us to reconsider our inherited definitions of church. On this new missional frontier, the old strategies focused solely on people or locations are incapable of reaching the growing share of the population. This is church out in the vast desert of nones and dones, the 60 percent that the inherited church will most likely never reach.

Fresh expressions are not *almost* church; they are churches in their own right. The people who make their spiritual home within them may never come back to the church compound. Some from Antioch may journey back to Jerusalem, but most will not.

As we speak and enflesh "the kingdom of God has come near" (Luke 10:11) through listening, loving/serving, forming community, and exploring discipleship, the practices themselves are transformed. The expression begins to live under the reign of Christ, which is reflected in the deep relational nature of the micro-community. The person of peace opens the gateway to authentic relationship and Christ is powerfully present as isolation is healed. A contextual church is forming among the native practices as Christians and not-yet-Christians live together. Sanctification is occurring gradually, as the community moves through the waves of grace.

The question becomes not, "How do we convert these people and their practices?" but "How is God working through these people and their practices?" Does this practice already point to Jesus? How can church be formed here?

Where is the isolation that needs healing through authentic withness? Who is the person of peace for this tribe? Pioneers go out in teams, inhabiting different relational spheres, searching for the already existing life-affirming tendencies, transforming the practices as we go.

Stage 6: Doing It Again

The final stage in the process is simply to repeat the process all over again. The potential for multiplication is huge. Fresh expressions are born pregnant. Typically, when someone within a fresh expression begins to turn over their whole lives to Christ, they begin to experience a call to plant another one with an unreached people group. As we see the ways that God uses ordinary people, we become encouraged that God use us in a similar way. We begin to hear statements like, "If _____ can do this, then so can I." The more time we spend in the community, the more connections we make, and the more the network expands. These missional green spaces multiply themselves and begin to transform the ecosystem at large.

Grafting

I want to suggest an important process and a few tools if the blended ecology way is going to truly work in local churches. For those futurefitting existing congregations in the blended ecology way, you may want to consider this a seventh stage. The team needs to find creative ways to keep the fresh expressions tethered to the anchor congregation. Like the structure of a Möbius strip, the life of the church should be flowing out into the community, and the life of the community flowing back into the church. This becomes a continuous open loop of cocreation.

While the focus of fresh expressions is not to revitalize the existing congregation, they provide a viable means for the local church to recover and retain a missional posture. In the summer of 2018 I had the opportunity to share and learn at the National Pioneer Gathering in Leicester, United Kingdom. This Leicester Diocese of the Church of England has been living into the mixed ecology for almost a decade. In the fresh expressions process, they are noticing the emergence of two distinct phenomenon they refer to as *edgelands* (missional enterprises that may or may not become "church") and *bridge backs* (fresh expressions in process that connect people back to an inherited church).

While the focus of a fresh expression is to become the fullness of the church in the larger communal ecosystem of first, second, and third places, some fresh expressions effectively connect people back to the local congregation for discipleship and connect people from the inherited church to people and culture outside of it. The bridge back is thus a two-way, not a one-way street. Furthermore, people that come to faith in the fresh expressions of church often find

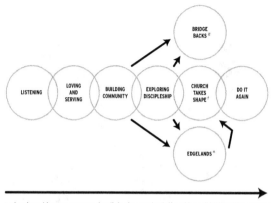

underpinned by prayer, on-going listening, and relationships with the wider church

their way back into inherited congregations as well. While some fresh expressions purists believe this muddies the missional waters, so to speak, I find no rational explanation for why we should not encourage and actively facilitate this kind of exchange.

Returning to Jesus' parable of the vineyard, a fitting analogy for this process is grafting (John 15:1–6). Again, grafting is an asexual propagation technique. In this process, a shoot system (called a scion) of one species is grafted on the root system (called a rootstock) of another. Paul takes up the language of grafting to describe the new composite reality of God's people as both Jew and Gentile, the deep roots and wild branches (Rom. 11:17–24).

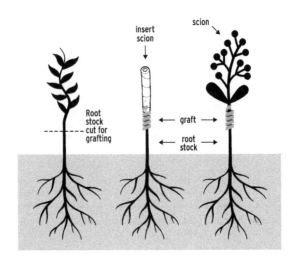

As we plant the scions (fresh expressions) we need to continually connect them back to the rootstock (inherited congregation). Michael Moynagh reminds us that organizations are sequences of conversations, in which any individual's contribution can catalyze change in the whole system. In organizational transformation language, grafting creates *feedback loops*, when outputs of a system are routed back as inputs thus forming a loop. Seemingly small inputs eventually magnify into large-scale transformation.[5]

Here are some simple grafting practices.

Telling Stories: Create platforms to share stories between emerging and inherited. Tell inherited stories in the emerging gatherings and vice versa.

Inviting: Invite people between the expressions to join each other.

Measure in Story: While we can record numbers of people, storytelling is the true metric.

Celebrate the Inherited Congregation: Celebrate the inherited congregation in the fresh expressions of church. Institutional church bashing sessions are not healthy for anyone.

Encourage Exploration of the Inherited Congregation: Encourage people meeting in the fresh expression to drop in on inherited church happenings.

Creating a Fourth Place: Create gatherings that are halfway between what someone would experience in a fresh expression and an attractional gathering. People bridging back into inherited congregations may not be ready for a full-on traditional worship experience. We need to create something in between that and a fresh expression. At Wildwood the fourth place is called New Life, a worship experience that features families with children of all ages together around tables for breakfast, sacred-in-the-secular music, dance breaks, social media moments, coffee toasts, and conversational presentations of Scripture.

Picnic Talk

People Map Exercise

This is a team listening exercise. Someone on your team is going to need to be the resident artist who will draw out the concepts on the map and bring it alive. As you see in the example below, they don't need to be skilled!

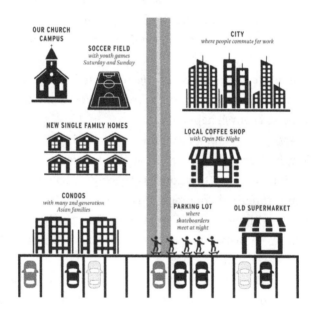

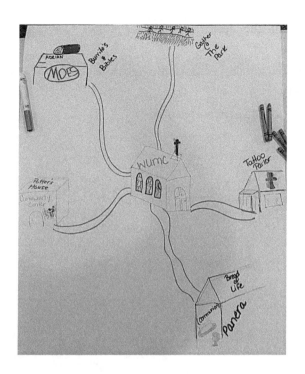

1. Draw your home base.

2. Draw out potential first, second, and third places where people gather.

3. Is there any place on the map where someone on the team goes frequently?

4. Do you have a person of peace in one of these locations already?

5. Prayerfully decide which possibilities have the most potential.

6. Who will take responsibility for the potential locations/networks/people?

7. What's the next logical step?

CHAPTER 8
Releasing

It is often this final move that churches in the inherited mode find the most difficult. Most of what I suggest here seemingly contradicts the prevailing logic of Christendom that has reigned for more than a thousand years. However, without releasing the priesthood of all believers to live into their identity as apostles, prophets, evangelists, pastors, and teachers (Eph. 4:11), cultivating new ecosystems in the blended ecology way will remain only a bold but impossible dream.

One of the most damaging realities of Christendom's assumed attractional-only mode is the professionalization of the clergy. Again, we have created an artificial ecosystem in churches where a paid minister is the center of the community, much like a Yellowstone without wolves. This model results from our consumeristic culture, in that church attendees (consumers) come to a central location to receive what professional ministers (producers) provide. A commoditization of religious goods and services, so to speak.

Beneath the levels of the bureaucratic sediment of Christendom lies an ugly truth: we've forgotten why we are here in the first place. Our why has been compressed under layers of rock, no longer a living and breathing source of joy and inspiration, but a fossilized relic of the distant past. When local churches lose their why, packing the pews becomes the default why of the congregation. This artificial purpose inadvertently creates pew potatoes: Christians who ride the pine from the sidelines, but never have an opportunity to get on the field. People in these congregations have been unwittingly programmed into a state of learned helplessness.

Learned Helplessness: A strong feeling of helplessness, accompanied by the belief that nothing one does matters.[1]

The attractional church mode unwittingly enables people to exist in this spiritually passive state of learned helplessness. Ultimately, long-term congregants become dependent on the church in much the same way one can become dependent on unhealthy relationships, substances, and instant gratification behaviors that ultimately short-circuit spiritual development and growth.

Whether we incessantly preach of a "church where everyone gets to play" or consistently stress the "body of Christ" and "priesthood of believers" concepts or not, the very structure and practices of the church form people in the opposite direction. Think about it. Our liturgies read "leader and people." The language of clergy and laity. The worship service itself is structured toward a single leader, who dominates most of the time with a professional presentation to the community.

In short, actions speak louder than words. We have been so indoctrinated in this way, we are largely unconscious of the ways we reinforce the passivity and helplessness of the people. No wonder so many ministers are frustrated, "I can't get my people to do anything!" We are training our people not to do anything with our actions, no matter what words we may choose.

Alan Hirsch has written prolifically on the "movemental" nature of the church, the necessity of apostolic leadership, new innovative practices that can advance multiplication, and recovering the fivefold ministry of Ephesians 4:11–13 in this manner: Apostles. Prophets. Evangelists. Shepherds. Teachers (APEST).

Hirsch explains the loss of the fivefold ministry from Ephesians 4:1–16 is in large part responsible for the massive decline of pastor-centered Christianity in the West.[2] In the primarily attractional model of Christendom where most of the population are already Christian and the basic assumption is that "if you build, they will come," the gift set of pastor and teacher is most needed. The pastor is tasked primarily with caring for those already in the flock. The teacher is tasked primarily with passing on the traditions of the faith from generation to generation.

Let's look at the passage and give brief working definitions for each these giftings:

> The gifts he gave were that some would be apostles, some prophets, some evangelists, some pastors and teachers, to equip the saints for the work of ministry, for building up the body of Christ, until all of us come to the unity of the faith and of the knowledge of the Son of God, to maturity, to the measure of the full stature of Christ. (Eph. 4:11–13)

Apostles: Those tasked with the extension of Christianity through direct mission and church planting. Their focus is moving the church outward, seeding the gospel in different host cultures.

Prophets: Those tasked with maintaining faithfulness to God among the people of God. They speak and embody God's now truth into the community. They are typically located on the edge of the center, both speaking a word into the community and to those outside of it.

Evangelists: Those naturally infectious persons who recruit others to the cause. They are outwardly focused, enlisting others into the movement and casting the seeds of the gospel throughout the world.

Shepherds (Pastors): Those tasked with nurturing the spiritual development and maintaining the communal health of the church. They serve the inward function of engendering the community in love toward God and each other.

Teachers: Those who pass along the wisdom and understanding bequeathed to the church. They, too, are focused internally on protecting and passing on the faith.

While the pastor/teacher roles are immensely important among the body of Christ, they are not sufficient alone to advance the body into the "full stature of Christ" (Eph. 4:13). We are so deeply engrained in this attractional way that it is extremely difficult to make any other proposal to long-term church attenders. The catch-all title of "pastor" being used for all clergy is a remnant of a declining Christendom model in the West.

All people are wired primarily in one of these personality categories. When we become Christians, God harnesses that potential for the greater good of building up the body.

Hirsch and others within the missional movement believe that not only were the apostles, prophets, and evangelists disregarded in the Christendom model, they were actively suppressed and silenced. They refer to this as "The Exiling of the APEs." In this scenario, all ministry has been forced into the predetermined molds of shepherd and teacher, with pastors and theologians the only legitimate leadership within the church.[3]

In *5Q: Reactivating the Original Intelligence and Capacity of the Body of Christ,* Hirsch calls for the "recalibration" of the church in the West. He reminds us that the great revolutions of history are not simply about discovering something new, but the radical recovery of something that was already there. He explains how a return to the fivefold ministry as a "primordial form" (one of the meta-ideas that serves as a foundational concept) is essential for the multiplication of the church.[4]

We could say the body of Christ consists of the five forms of the APEST at a cellular level. Each person is a cell in the body, of which Jesus is the head.

Identifying the Wolves—Pioneers

The first step of releasing begins with identifying the apostles, prophets, evangelists, pastors, and teachers already in our congregations. We are looking specifically for the pioneering-type persons, the wolves in our Yellowstone metaphor.

Today, there is an incredible array of resources designed to identify and assess the various equippers in the local church. At Wildwood, we regularly hold what we call "body-building gatherings." As the body of Christ, we acknowledge each of us serves specific functions within that body (1 Cor. 12:27–30). We focus on our call as the "priesthood" of all believers (1 Peter 2:4–10). Each of our leaders takes a couple of assessments, including spiritual gifts, APEST (Apostles, Prophets, Evangelists, Shepherds, Teachers), and Clifton StrengthsFinder. We find it helpful to combine the use of a secular tool with spiritual gift assessments. It is incredible how the different assessments often validate their reliability and magnify the obvious gifting of the person.

We enter those results into a spreadsheet and use team-building resources to understand and develop each other's unique roles.

Two Essential Questions

At Wildwood, as the decline began to reverse, one of the lessons we learned was to catch people as they were entering the life of the church and harness their passions and relational networks.

We frequently ask of every person, two essential questions:

1. What are your hobbies, interests, passions; what do you love to do in your spare time?
2. What networks of people outside the church are you involved with? What groups do you participate in? (ex. quilting, golf, fitness, bingo, clubs, civic organizations, communities, etc.)

What we have discovered is that almost every person coming into the life of our church has a passion or hobby. Many times, people are already spending their time and energy in some practice; it only takes a simple remix to create a fresh expression. When we fuse that passion with the potential for a fresh expression of church, the results are explosive.

For instance, back to the example of my friend Larry at the dog park—remember the one with the bad taste in hats? He responded to me that, "I don't really have any hobbies. I bring my dog to the dog park." Larry has a huge labradoodle named Rocky that he brings to the park often. So I investigated this, "Larry, so you go to the same dog park every week at essentially the same time, you know people there, and you have relationship with them?"

This is one of those shared practices we spoke of earlier, of the mobile and networked society, gathering and doing life in the flows. People gather in dog parks and form community around their common love for dogs. When you get to the park, all the relational components are already present. People gather, talk, and connect in the same space, sometimes multiple times per week. Do you see how ingredients of church are already there? Now, my little black pug, Vader, and Larry's giant white labradoodle, Rocky, gather to have church together every week at Paws of Praise.

Doctor Renee was a certified Amrit Yoga instructor. Her passion is now a fresh expression called Yoga Therapy Church. Denise is an avid runner who has relationship with a whole network of runners; her passion has now been reborn as a fresh expression called Church 3.1. Krista is a veteran beautician, now she is the pastor of Shear Love at Soul

Salon. Mojo was a tattoo artist; his passion and connections helped us launch Tattoo Parlor Church. Do you see where this is going? Fresh expressions is a vehicle to release the priesthood of all believers—the apostles, prophets, evangelists, pastors, and teachers—that once filled our pews to be a missionary force for revealing the kingdom.

Furthermore, the initial training is minimal; it's more about discovering and releasing. We have embraced the Fresh Expressions UK model of low initial training, high ongoing support.[5] Failing forward faster.

Releasing the Wolves

One of my mentors and personal Master Yoda, Walter Edwards, says, "If you want to know how to catch a rabbit, talk to a hound dog with some hair in their teeth." Hound dogs possess a keen olfactory sense; they can smell rabbits from a mile away. They are hardwired to pursue and catch rabbits. There are people in our congregations who are hound dogs. They are designed to seek and find those that have separated themselves from God. Many times, in local churches, there is no viable pipeline for them to exercise their gifts. We need to release them.

Initially a no-wolves scenario seemed like a good idea at Yellowstone; it protected the vulnerable, less predatory animals like the deer. Most churches are perpetuating that kind of artificial scenario. We do such a good job pulling people so deeply into the life of the church that the church becomes their life, and they lose contact with any non-Christian friends. In our desire to create little colonies of holiness, we become a gated community where one needs a special behavioral access code to gain entrance. The longer congregations exist, the more pronounced this reality becomes. This is clearly evidenced by the church life cycle.

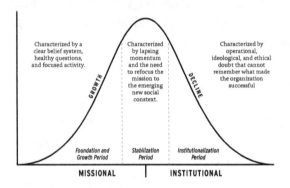

Older congregations typically grow more inwardly focused. A congregation not dealing with the messy sin-brokenness of the people in the community just outside their facility walls or the often swept-under-the-rug sins of their members is an artificial scenario. Some scholars have called this the "institutional" period.

To experience revitalization, older churches are going to have to start planting new churches to reverse this trend in the form of an "S curve." This is the power of the blended ecology way; it allows churches with significant history in communities to become multi-site. While the fresh expressions may not resemble the inherited form, it allows churches to reach people in the community the traditional church cannot. The key to success here is not expecting more from already exhausted clergy, but releasing the people of God.

I have seen adopting the fresh expressions approach and restructuring in the blended ecology way revitalize congregations beyond even the difficult transformation point as illustrated below.

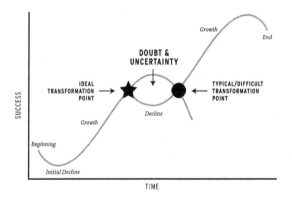

Releasing the wolves will disrupt the toxic loop, create missional mess, establish new grazing patterns, and redirect the rivers. The blended ecology allows us to recover our why and rediscover our core story—a vision where wolves and deer can coexist. We must nurture that deeper story of the "priesthood" of all believers (1 Peter 2:4–10) and dismantle the "professional minister" idea of late-twentieth-century corporate North America. That narrative is no longer authentic or viable. We need to recover the APEST design of Ephesians 4:11. In this blended mode the existing facility becomes a missional sending point, where everyone has a role.

We need to utilize our pioneers, supporters, and permission givers, and create a new relational ecosystem. There will be blood, death, and sacrifice before the new rivers can flow.

Small Changes = Massive Impact

The key to cultivating new ecosystems is "dream big, start small." This process is all about small, continuous, disruptive changes. Your team must understand themselves as a kind of keystone species in the food chain. The new environment we are seeking to create in a revitalization context is the blended ecology. Let's return to the controlling image: a tree thriving in the desert, and in its shade is the tapestry of color, new flowers, and life-forms thriving in the rootball. These organisms of deep roots and wild branches are blending together.

This is a new ecosystem amidst a barren death-dealing context. The blended organisms are giving life to each other in a symbiotic relationship as fresh life, fresh oxygen, and fresh spaces are being generated.

The blended ecology is not created through a single act of massive change. It does not take shape by uprooting the existing tree or chopping it up into firewood. In fact, there are three major areas to focus activity to produce the new blended ecosystem:

1. Caring, trimming, and fertilizing the existing tree.
2. Planting, cultivating, and fertilizing the fresh life-forms.
3. Grafting the old and new life-forms together.

These are small changes with massive implications for the ecosystem. The tree will die without appropriate care. If the tree dies, the new life-forms cannot exist without its shade and the nutrients of the complex root system. For the ecosystem cultivators, this is a delicate balance. We must think process; thus, revitalization is best understood more in the organic language of *trophic cascades* than referring to programs/products.

While competence in organizational leadership is necessary, what is imperative is combining it with relational and adaptive leadership skills. The ecosystem is a complex network of life; there are extraneous variables that cannot be anticipated or at times even measured. When the wolves were introduced back into Yellowstone, no one could have anticipated the massive impact: the growth of trees, a renewed abundance of life-forms, the reshaping of the environment itself, and the changing of the rivers.

When cultivating a new ecosystem, it is essential to remember, "I planted [the seed], Apollos watered, but God gave the growth" (1 Cor. 3:6). The only one who really has the power to bring dead things back to life is God. We can do everything in our power, but in a revitalization, we are completely reliant upon the power of God. Fortunately, God creates new ecosystems through the process of the trophic cascades.

I find the concept of trophic cascades permeating Scripture. God uses the small voices, small people, and small beginnings to unleash the power of resurrection and transform the universe. Small acts of love have massive kingdom potential to create new ecosystems. "Cup[s] of cold water" (Matt. 10:40–42) release the trophic cascades that become the river of life in the new creation (Rev. 22). As we saw earlier, ecosystems become sick when artificial conditions are forced upon them. God is all about creating and re-creating new ecosystems.

These small acts must be embodied in our daily living. It was the way the first Christians lived that God used to grow the church from an oppressed minority to a massive world-changing movement. The instinctual rhythms of their relational being—the day-to-day lives of these people—were the attraction to outsiders, not buildings, rituals, and forceful oratory demonstrations.

The early model of the church was the emerging model. The church scattered, with very few centers where the gathered model was a reality.

We find ourselves on a new frontier where the blended way is most appropriate to reaching new people. Most people from upcoming generations in our post-everything context are not going to show up at our steeples and cathedrals on a Sunday morning. No matter how compelling our preaching, no matter how professional our music, no matter how pristine our buildings, the largest demographic of our population is simply not going to show up.

We must release the keystone species to catalyze trophic cascades in our communal ecosystems. Local churches can transform the larger ecosystem and provide places where people can be released into the flows of a networked society. We can join the Spirit in planting the seeds in the green spaces, and futurefit this earth with the life of heaven now.

It is my deepest prayer for you that your churches and communities will experience an alternative ending to the prominent themes of decline and closure. Good-bye for now, until we once again gather together for a picnic at the tree of life in the urban garden of new creation.

See you at the tree, my friends!

Picnic Talk

(For this picnic, locate some spiritual gifts assessments and have each team member share their results. There are free APEST inventories available on the Internet.)

1. Do you see the state of spiritual learned helplessness described here in your church? Why or why not?

2. What percentage of the work of ministry do you guess the pastor of your church does? Do you feel you have a team-based leadership model in your church?

3. How do you see the priesthood of all believers at work in your congregation? What small behavior changes in the keystone species could release more people to operate in their giftings?

4. Let each person share their assessment results and responses to these questions. What was your highest APEST score? Do you agree with the results? Why or why not?

5. Now, let each member of the team comment about how you see those giftings in each other. Where do you think would be the most effective place for your team members to serve?

6. What fresh expressions of church could you see yourself cultivating? Do you have a passion or hobby you could

see planting a church around? What networks, clubs, or organizations do you have access to?

7. Do you feel like you are a pioneer, supporter, or permission giver? Why?

Sources

Backert, Chris. Collected from a presentation delivered before the Society of Church Growth on October 20, 2017 at Asbury Theological Seminary.

Bolger, Ryan K. 2007. "Practice Movements in Global Information Culture: Looking Back to McGavran and Finding a Way Forward." *Missiology* 35, no. 2: 181–93. (2007), 188.

Bolsinger, Tod E. *Canoeing the Mountains: Christian Leadership in Uncharted Territory*. Downers Grove, IL: IVP Books, 2016.

Castells, Manuel. *The Rise of the Network Society*. Oxford Malden, MA: Blackwell Publishers, 2000.

Cray, Graham, Ian Mobsby, and Aaron Kennedy. *Fresh Expressions of Church and the Kingdom of God*. Norwich: Canterbury Press, 2012.

Cray, Graham. *Mission-shaped Church: Church Planting and Fresh Expressions in a Changing Context*. New York, NY: Seabury Books, 2010.

Estes, J. A., and John Terborgh. *Trophic Cascades: Predators, Prey, and the Changing Dynamics of Nature*. Washington [DC]: Island Press, 2010.

Fosner, Verlon. *Dinner Church: Building Bridges by Breaking Bread*. Franklin, TN: Seedbed Publishing, 2017.

Fujimura, Makoto. *Culture Care: Reconnecting with Beauty for Our Common Life*. New York: Fujimura Institute, 2014.

Fully Charged "The Sustainable City" on YouTube at https://www.youtube.com/watch?v=WCKz8ykyI2E&t=630s.

Gaze, Sally. *Mission-shaped and Rural: Growing Churches in the Countryside*. London: Church House Publishing, 2006.

Hirsch, Alan. *5Q: Reactivating the Original Intelligence and Capacity of the Body of Christ*. USA: 100M, 2017.

Hirsch, Alan, Tim Catchim, and Mike Breen. *The Permanent Revolution: Apostolic Imagination and Practice for the 21st Century Church*. San Francisco: Jossey-Bass, 2012.

"How Wolves Change Rivers" on YouTube at https://youtu.be/ysa5OBhXz-Q.

Luz Grácio, Ana Helena, and Cátia Rijo. "Design thinking in the scope of strategic and collaborative design." *Strategic Design Research Journal* 10, no. 1 (January 2017): 30–35.

Magle, Seth B., and Lisa M. Angeloni. 2011. "Effects of Urbanization on the Behaviour of a Keystone Species." Behaviour 148 (1): 31–54. doi:10.1163/000579510X545810.

Maier, Steven F., and Martin E. P. Seligman. 2016. "Learned Helplessness at Fifty: Insights From Neuroscience." *Psychological Review* 123, no. 4: 349-367. http://dx.doi.org/10.1037/rev0000033.

Merkle, J. A., D. R. Stahler, and D. W. Smith. "Merkle, J. A., D. R. Interference competition between gray wolves and coyotes in Yellowstone National Park." *Journal of Zoology* 87, no. 1: 56–63., 2009.

Moynagh, Michael. *Church in Life: Emergence, Ecclesiology and Entrepreneurship*. London, UK: SCM Press, 2017.

Nelstrop, Louise, and Martyn Percy. *Evaluating Fresh Expressions: Explorations in Emerging Church: Responses to the Changing Face of Ecclesiology in the Church of England.* Norwich: Canterbury Press, 2008.

Oldenburg, Ray. *The Great Good Place: Cafés, Coffee Shops, Bookstores, Bars, Hair Salons, and Other Hangouts at the Heart of a Community.* New York Berkeley, CA: Marlowe Distributed by Publishers Group West, 1999.

Putnam, Robert D. *Bowling Alone: The Collapse and Revival of American Community.* New York: Simon & Schuster, 2000.

Sarasvathy, Saras D., *What Makes Entrepreneurs Entrepreneurial?* https://dx.doi.org/.

Sinek, Simon. *Start with Why: How Great Leaders Inspire Everyone to Take Action.* New York: Portfolio, 2009.

Sweet, Leonard I. *From Tablet to Table: Where Community Is Found and Identity Is Formed.* Colorado Springs, CO: NavPress, 2014.

Taylor, Paul. *The Next America: Boomers, Millennials, and the Looming Generational Showdown.* New York: Public Affairs: Public Affairs, 2015.

Wheatley, Margaret J. *Leadership and the New Science: Discovering Order in a Chaotic World.* San Francisco: Berrett-Koehler Publishers, 1999.

Notes

Trailer

1. Sally Gaze, *Mission-shaped and Rural: Growing Churches in the Countryside* (London: Church House Publishing, 2006), xviii.
2. Chris Backert, From a presentation before the Society of Church Growth on October 20, 2017, at Asbury Theological Seminary.

Chapter One

1. Paul Taylor, *The Next America: Boomers, Millennials, and the Looming Generational Showdown* (New York: Public Affairs, 2015), 51–52.
2. Ibid., 39.
3. Ibid., 44.
4. Graham Cray, *Mission-shaped Church: Church Planting and Fresh Expressions of Church in a Changing Context* (New York, NY: Seabury Books, 2010), 3–4.

5. Robert D. Putnam, *Bowling Alone: The Collapse and Revival of American Community* (New York: Simon & Schuster, 2000), 71.

6. Taylor, *The Next America*, 163.

7. Ibid., 173.

8. Cray, *Mission-shaped Church*, 4.

9. Manuel Castells, *The Rise of the Network Society* (Oxford Malden, MA: Blackwell Publishers, 2000), xvii–xviii.

10. Ibid., 442.

11. Ryan K. Bolger, "Practice Movements in Global Information Culture: Looking Back to McGavran and Finding a Way Forward," *Missiology* 35, no. 2: 181–93. (2007), 188.

Chapter Two

1. Graham Cray, *The Mission-shaped Church: Church Planting and Fresh Expressions in a Changing Context* (New York, NY: Seabury Books, 2010), x.

Chapter Three

1. Ray, Oldenburg, *The Great Good Place: Cafés, Coffee Shops, Bookstores, Bars, Hair Salons, and Other Hangouts at the Heart of a Community* (New York Berkeley, CA: Marlowe Publishers Group West, 1999), 16.

2. You can watch the *Fully Charged* documentary on Masdar City, "The Sustainable City" on YouTube at https://youtu.be/WCKz8ykyI2E.

3. Graham Cray, *Mission-shaped Church: Church Planting and Fresh Expressions in a Changing Context* (New York, NY: Seabury Books, 2010), 100.
4. Ibid., 28.

Chapter Four

1. Paul Taylor, *The Next America: Boomers, Millennials, and the Looming Generational Showdown* (New York: Public Affairs, 2015), 58.

Chapter Five

1. J. A. Merkle, D. R. Stahler, and D. W. Smith, "Merkle, J. A., D. R. Interference competition between gray wolves and coyotes in Yellowstone National Park," *Journal of Zoology* 87, no. 1:56–63, 2009: 57.
2. J. A. Estes and John Terborgh, "Trophic Cascades: Predators, Prey, and the Changing Dynamics of Nature" (Washington, DC: Island Press, 2010).
3. "How Wolves Change Rivers" YouTube at https://youtu.be/ysa5OBhXz-Q.
4. Seth B. Magle and Lisa M. Angeloni, "Effects of Urbanization on the Behaviour of a Keystone Species," *Behaviour* 148 (1): 31–54. (2011) doi:10 .1163/000579510X545810.
5. Simon Sinek, *Start with Why: How Great Leaders Inspire Everyone to Take Action* (New York: Portfolio, 2009), 39, 213.

6. Margaret J. Wheatley, *Leadership and the New Science: Discovering Order in a Chaotic World* (San Francisco: Berrett-Koehler Publishers, 1999), 24.

7. Saras D. Sarasvathy, "What Makes Entrepreneurs Entrepreneurial?" 2. https://www.effectuation.org/sites /default/files/research_papers/what-makes-entrepre neurs-entrepreneurial-sarasvathy_0.pdf.

8. Tod E. Bolsinger, *Canoeing the Mountains: Christian Leadership in Uncharted Territory* (Downers Grove, IL: IVP Books, an imprint of InterVarsity Press, 2016), 36.

9. Michael Moynagh, *Church in Life: Emergence, Ecclesiology and Entrepreneurship* (London, UK: SCM Press, 2017), 34.

10. Ibid., 24–25

11. Ibid.

12. Bolsinger, *Canoeing the Mountains*, 82.

Chapter Six

1. Alan Hirsch, Tim Catchim, and Mike Breen, *The Permanent Revolution: Apostolic Imagination and Practice for the 21st Century Church* (San Francisco, CA: Jossey-Bass, 2012), 7.

2. Makoto Fujimura, *Culture Care: Reconnecting with Beauty for Our Common Life* (New York: Fujimura Institute, 2014), 39.

3. Ibid.

4. Grácio Luz, Ana Helena, and Cátia Rijo, "Design Thinking in the Scope of Strategic and Collaborative

Design," *Strategic Design Research Journal* 10, no. 1 (January 2017): 30–31.

Chapter Seven

1. Verlon Fosner, *Dinner Church: Building Bridges by Breaking Bread* (Franklin, TN: Seedbed Publishing, 2017), 107–8.
2. Tod E. Bolsinger, *Canoeing the Mountains: Christian Leadership in Uncharted Territory* (Downers Grove, IL: IVP Books, 2016), 191.
3. Leonard I. Sweet, *From Tablet to Table: Where Community Is Found and Identity Is Formed* (Colorado Springs, CO: NavPress, 2014), 4–5.
4. Graham Cray, Ian Mobsby, and Aaron Kennedy, *Fresh Expressions of Church and the Kingdom of God* (Norwich: Canterbury Press, 2012), 24.
5. Michael Moynagh, *Church in Life: Emergence, Ecclesiology and Entrepreneurship* (London, UK: SCM Press, 2017), 22–23.

Chapter Eight

1. Steven F. Maier and Martin E. P. Seligman, "Learned Helplessness at Fifty: Insights from Neuroscience," *Psychological Review* 123, no. 4: 349–67. (2016) 349 http://dx.doi.org/10.1037/rev0000033.
2. Alan Hirsch, Tim Catchim, and Mike Breen, *The Permanent Revolution: Apostolic Imagination and Practice for the 21st Century Church* (San Francisco: Jossey-Bass, 2012), 5–9.

3. Ibid., 17.

4. Alan Hirsch, *5Q: Reactivating the Original Intelligence and Capacity of the Body of Christ* (USA: 100M, 2017), 19.

5. Louise Nelstrop and Martyn Percy, *Evaluating Fresh Expressions: Explorations in Emerging Church: Responses to the Changing Face of Ecclesiology in the Church of England* (Norwich: Canterbury Press, 2008), 48.

1833 SE Camino
Rew Av.
Stuart, FL.
34994-

CPSIA information can be obtained
at www.ICGtesting.com
Printed in the USA
LVHW010700190822
726128LV00003B/7

9 781628 246223